Foreword

The Hidden Places is a collection of easy to use travel guides taking you, in this instance, on a relaxed but informative tour of Northumberland & Durham or to use its ancient name, The Kingdom of Northumbria. Northumberland is one of England's loveliest counties with its National Park, Cheviot Hills and Kielder Water and Forest. It also has an attractive coastline containing the historic Holy Island of Lindisfarne as well as Hadrian's Roman Wall and many historic castles. County Durham not only possesses some beautiful and unspoilt landscape such as the Durham Dales but is blessed with the historic city of Durham, impressive castles, and a deep industrial heritage.

This edition of *The Hidden Places of Northumberland and Durham* is published *in full colour*. All *Hidden Places* titles will now be published in colour which will ensure that readers can properly appreciate the attractive scenery and impressive places of interest in these counties and, of course, in the rest of the British Isles. We do hope that you like the new format.

Our books contain a wealth of interesting information on the history, the countryside, the towns and villages and the more established places of interest in the county. But they also promote the more secluded and little known visitor attractions and places to stay, eat and drink many of which are easy to miss unless you know exactly where you are going.

We include hotels, inns, restaurants, public houses, teashops, various types of accommodation, historic houses, museums, gardens, garden centres, craft centres and many other attractions throughout Northumberland and Durham, all of which are comprehensively indexed. Most places are accompanied by an attractive photograph and are easily located by using the map at the beginning of each chapter. We do not award merit marks or rankings but concentrate on describing the more interesting, unusual or unique features of each place with the aim of making the reader's stay in the local area an enjoyable and stimulating experience.

Whether you are visiting the area for business or pleasure or in fact are living in the county we do hope that you enjoy reading and using this book. We are always interested in what readers think of places covered (or not covered) in our guides so please do not hesitate to use the reader reaction forms provided to give us your considered comments. We also welcome any general comments which will help us improve the guides themselves. Finally if you are planning to visit any other corner of the British Isles we would like to refer you to the list of other *Hidden Places* titles to be found at the rear of the book and to the Travel Publishing website at www.travelpublishing.co.uk.

Travel Publishing

Regional Map

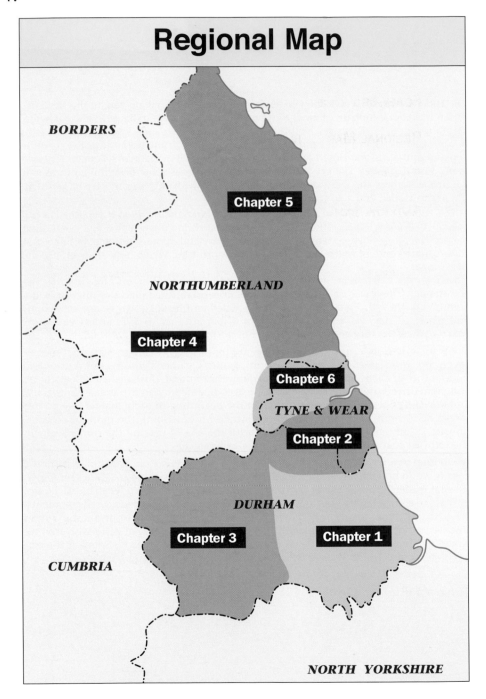

BORDERS

Chapter 5

NORTHUMBERLAND

Chapter 4

Chapter 6

TYNE & WEAR

Chapter 2

DURHAM

Chapter 3

Chapter 1

CUMBRIA

NORTH YORKSHIRE

Contents

Authors Note

Of all the areas of England, the North East has changed most in local government terms. In the last 30 years or so, boundaries have come and gone, county councils formed then wound up, and new unitary authorities established. Before 1974, there were only two counties - Northumberland and Durham. Then local government reorganisation introduced two new counties - Tyne and Wear, which encompassed parts of both Northumberland and County Durham, and Cleveland, which also took in parts of County Durham, but included parts of North Yorkshire as well. Towns and cities such as Sunderland, Newcastle-upon Tyne, Hartlepool and Stockton-on-Tees suddenly found themselves removed from their traditional counties and placed within the boundaries of these new ones.

Then, some time later, Tyne and Wear was formally wound up as an administrative unit, though the towns and cities within it were not returned to their former counties, but remained in the Tyne and Wear area. In 1997 it was Cleveland's turn. In this case, even the name disappeared, to be replaced by an area, or sub region, known as Tees Valley. All the towns within it, such as Hartlepool, Darlington and Stockton became "unitary authorities" and found themselves in the curious position of not being within a county at all.

But old loyalties have never died. I lived in the area for some time, and know that many people from Hartlepool, for instance, still considered their town to be within County Durham even though they were nominally within Cleveland at the time. The same with the people of Sunderland, Gateshead and South Shields - Durhamites all, as a colleague once told me, even though they were within Tyne and Wear. And even today many of the people of Newcastle and North Tyneside still consider themselves to be Northumbrians to the core, and the citizens of Darlington and Stockton, in their heart of hearts, still consider their towns to be within County Durham.

In laying out this book, I have taken my lead from the majority of people who live in the area, and have ignored present day political boundaries. The ones I have followed are the pre-1974 ones, where Northumberland was bounded on the north by Scotland and on the south by the Tyne for part of its length, and County Durham's northern boundary was the Tyne, and the Tees separated it from Yorkshire.

James Gracie

1 Central and Southern County Durham

County Durham's prosperity was founded on coalmining, and nowhere is this more apparent than in parts of Central and South Durham. Coal has been mined here for centuries, and no doubt the monks of Durham, Jarrow

Durham Cathedral, Castle and Boathouse

and all the other abbeys and priories in the area exploited the rich seams that underpin the landscape.

It wasn't until the 18th century, however, that the industry was established on a commercial basis. When the railways came along in the early 19th century, the industry prospered. It created great wealth for the land-owners, and sometimes great misery for the miners. The explosion in Trimdon Grange Colliery in 1882, for instance, claimed the lives of 74 miners - some of them no more than boys. And in May 1951, 81 men were killed by an underground explosion in Easington Colliery on the coast.

Now that the industry has all but disappeared, the scars it created are being swept away. Spoil heaps have been cleared or grassed over, pit heads demolished and old industrial sites tidied up. The colliery villages, some with names that bring a smile to the face, such as Pity Me, Shiney Row, No Place, Bearpark, Sunniside, Quebec and Toronto, are still there however -

tight-knit communities that retain an old-style sense of belonging and sharing. But even in the most unpre-possessing of villages there are delightful surprises, such as the almost perfect Saxon church at Escomb.

Coal may have been king, but County Durham's countryside has always supported an important

Prebends Bridge, Durham

farming industry, and Central and South Durham still retains a gentle landscape of fields, woodland, streams and narrow country lanes. It stretches from the coast in the east to the Pennines in the west, and from the old border with Yorkshire in the south to the edge of the Tyne and the Wear conurbations in the north. Within this area there are picturesque villages, cottages, grand houses, museums, snug pubs, old churches and castles aplenty.

Then there's the coastline. This too has been cleaned up, and now an 11-mile coastal footpath snakes through the district of Easington from Seaham Hall Beach in the north to Crimdon Park in the south. Most of it is along clifftops with spectacular views down onto the beaches. This coastal area has been designated as a National Nature Reserve, with some Sites of Special Scientific Interest along the way.

The Romans marched along **Dere Street** in County Durham, and in the 9th and 10th centuries holy men carried the body of St Cuthbert with them as they sought a place of refuge from the marauding Vikings. And, of course, the railways were born in the county in 1825, with the opening of the famous **Stockton and Darlington Railway**.

Dominating the whole area is the city of Durham - surely one of Europe's finest small cities. A whole week could be spent there without seeing all it has to offer. It was here, in 1832, that

Central Keep, Durham Castle

England's third great university was established.

And there are the towns of Darlington, Stockton-on-Tees, Hartlepool and Bishop Auckland to explore. All of these places were at one time within the borders of the county, but local government reorganisation placed two of them - Hartlepool and Stockton-on-Tees - in the upstart county of Cleveland. Now that Cleveland itself is no more, they, along with Darlington, are unitary authorities, and, strictly speaking, not part of County Durham at all, though old loyalties still exist.

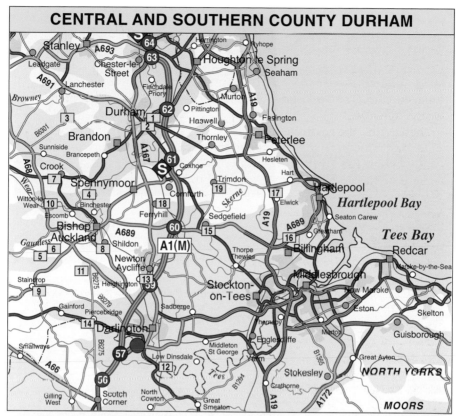

CENTRAL AND SOUTHERN COUNTY DURHAM

© MAPS IN MINUTES ™ (1999)

PLACES TO STAY, EAT, DRINK AND SHOP

FARNLEY TOWER

The Avenue, Durham City DH1 4DX
Tel: 0191 375 0011
Fax: 0191 383 9694
e-mail enquiries@farnley-tower.co.uk
website www.farnley-tower.co.uk

Farnley Tower can be found on a quiet street in the heart of Durham City. This impressive, stone-built, country house was originally a gentleman's residence, dating back to the early 19th century, and just two years ago was opened by John Khan as a luxurious guest house.

The whole building is decorated and furnished to the highest of standards with everything from the bed linen to the crockery being of the finest quality. Each of the 12 guest rooms has been individually styled and designed using a range of traditional colours and fabrics. Each has en-suite facilities and offers guests a direct dial telephone with modem socket, colour TV, hairdryer, ironing board with iron, and refreshment tray. Residents can enjoy a freshly cooked breakfast in the downstairs dining room with everything from the full cooked English breakfast to the fresh fruit platter being prepared using the finest of local produce.

The house enjoys fine panoramic views over the city and is surrounded by pleasant gardens which are ideal for relaxing with an afternoon cup of tea or early evening drink. Guests can also make use of the fully licensed lounge bar. A number of visitors return again and again to this most delightful of establishments which is ideal for a weekend break, touring base or for business use.

MOUNT OSWALD MANOR AND GOLF COURSE

South Road, Durham City, DH1 3TQ
Tel: 0191 3867527 Fax: 0191386097
e-mail: information@mountoswald.co.uk www:mountosawld.co.uk

Just two miles south of historic Durham City, off the A177, is **Mount Oswald Manor and Golf Course**. This fine 18-hole golf course is conveniently located not far from the city and is readily accessible to visitors to the area. Set within the extensive grounds of Mount Oswald Manor the course is open to the public, groups are also welcome by prior arrangement, and green fees are very reasonable. Clubs and trolleys are available for hire.

The impressive Georgian Manor House dates from 1800 and enjoys a picturesque setting surrounded by exquisite gardens and rolling countryside. The delightful house is well maintained and pleasantly furnished while retaining a friendly welcoming atmosphere. Open to the public each day, visitors can enjoy a refreshing drink in the bar area or a bite to eat in the delightful restaurant. Food is offered from a wide ranging menu of tasty meals and snacks complemented by a daily specials board. Extensive wine lists enable guests to select a fine wine to enjoy with their meal.

The large house also includes a number of function suites which are available for hire for business meetings, wedding receptions and private parties. The rooms vary in size to suit a variety of occasions and the room hire rates are very reasonable. Many of the function rooms, together with the restaurant and bar, enjoy fine views over the golf course and surrounding countryside.

DURHAM CITY

Arriving in Durham by train, the visitor is presented with what must be one of the most breathtaking urban views in Europe. Towering over the tumbling roofs of the city is the magnificent bulk of **Durham Cathedral**, and, close by, the majestic **Durham Castle**.

No visit to the city is complete without time spent at the cathedral. It is third only to Canterbury and York in ecclesiastical significance, but excels them in architectural splendour. Quite simply, it is the finest and grandest example of Norman architecture in Europe. This was the powerbase of the wealthy Prince Bishops of Durham who once exercised king-like powers in an area known the Palatinate of Durham.

Durham Cathedral and River

These powers were vested in them by William I, and they could administer civil and criminal law; they could issue pardons, hold their own parliament, mint their own money, create baronetcies, and give market charters. They could even raise their own army. Though these powers were never exercised in later years, they continued in theory right up until 1836, when the last of the Prince Bishops, Bishop William Van Mildert, died. The Palatinate Courts, however, were only abolished in 1971. It is little wonder that the County Council now proudly presents the county to visitors as "The Land of the Prince Bishops".

Even more significantly, in the cathedral are the tombs of two of the greatest figures of the early Christian church in England: the remarkable St Cuthbert (AD635-687), shepherd saint of Northumbria, and the Venerable Bede (AD673-735), saint, scholar and Britain's first and pre-eminent historian.

The cathedral owes its origin to the monks of Lindisfarne, who, in AD875, fled from Viking attacks, taking with them the coffin of St Cuthbert. In AD883 they settled at Chester-le-Street. However, further Viking raids in AD980 caused them to move once more, and they eventually arrived at a more easily defended site about ten miles to the south, where the River Wear makes a wide loop round a rocky outcrop. Here, in Durham, they built the "White Church", where St Cuthbert's remains were finally laid to rest.

The founder of the present cathedral, however, was a Norman, William de St Carileph, or Calais, Bishop of Durham from 1081 to 1096. He brought to the White Church not only holy relics but, in 1083, a group of monks and scholars from Monkwearmouth and Jarrow.

William fled to Normandy in 1088, having been accused of plotting against William Rufus, but returned in 1091 after a pardon, determined to replace the little church with a building of the scale and style of the splendid new churches he saw being built in France at that time. In August 1093 the foundation stones were laid, a witness being King Malcolm III of Scotland, famed as the soldier who slew Macbeth in battle.

The main part of the great building was erected in a mere 40 years, but over ensuing centuries each generation has added magnificent work or superb detail of its own, such as the 14th century Episcopal Throne, said to be the highest in Christendom, and the Neville Screen. Yet the impregnable fortress-like quality of the cathedral, with its famous carved columns, retains a visual splendour that makes it a very special place. Even so, nothing is more moving than the simple fragments of carved wood which survive from St Cuthbert's coffin, made for the saint's body in AD698 and carried around the North of England by his devoted followers before being laid to rest in the mighty cathedral. The fragments are now kept in the **Treasures of St Cuthbert Exhibition**, within the cathedral, with examples of the Prince Bishops' own silver coins.

Durham Castle, sharing the same rocky peninsula and standing close to the cathedral, was founded in 1072 and belonged to the Prince Bishops. Such was the impregnability of the site that Durham was one of the few towns in Northumbria that was never captured by the Scots using force. Among the castle's most impressive features are the Chapel, dating from 1080, and the Great Hall, which was built in the middle of the 13th century. Though the Keep was

Durham Castle

restored in Victorian times, it remains a remarkable building in its own right.

The importance of the whole area surrounding the cathedral and castle was recognised in 1987, when it was designated a UNESCO World Heritage Site.

The Castle is now used as a hall of residence for the students of Durham University and is only open to the public at limited times. But students and visitors should beware - the castle is reputedly haunted by no less than three ghosts. One is supposed to be of Jane, wife of Bishop Van Mildert, and takes the form of the top half of a woman in 19th-century dress. She glides along the Norman Gallery, leaving the scent of apple blossom in her wake. A second spirit is of university tutor Frederick

Copeman, who, in 1880, threw himself off the tower of the cathedral. His ghost is said to haunt his former room off the Norman Gallery. A further apparition, which has been seen at various locations within the castle, is a cowled monk.

The university - the third to be established in England - was founded in 1832 by Bishop Van Mildert. In 1837 it moved into Durham Castle, though today its many buildings are scattered throughout the south of the city.

The rest of Durham reflects the long history of the castle and cathedral it served. There are winding streets, such as Saddler Street and Silver Street, whose names reveal their medieval origin, the ancient Market Place, elegant Georgian houses, particularly around South Bailey, and quiet courts and alleyways. There are also many churches, such as **St Nicholas's Church** in the Market Place, **St Margaret of Antioch Church** in Crossgate, **St Mary le Bow Church** in North Bailey (now **The Durham Heritage Centre and Museum**, which is well worth visiting), **St Giles Church** in Gilesgate, **St Oswald's Church** in Church Street and **St Mary the Less Church** in South Bailey, which shows

that, in medieval times, this was a great place of pilgrimage.

In the western outskirts of the city, and straddling the A167, is the site of the **Battle of Neville's Cross**, fought in 1346 between Scotland and England. The Scottish army was heavily defeated, and the Scottish king, David 11, was taken prisoner. A leaflet has been produced which guides visitors round the site.

A favourite and famous walk past castle and cathedral follows the footpaths which run through the woodlands on each bank of the River Wear, around the great loop. You can begin either at Framwellgate Bridge or Elvet Bridge. The path along the inside of the loop goes past **The Old Fulling Mill**, sited below the cathedral, which now houses an archaeological museum containing material from excavations in and around the city. If walking isn't to your taste you can take a cruise along the river from Elvet Bridge.

The **DLI Museum and Durham Art Gallery** at Aykley Heads has been totally refurbished. It tells the story of the county's own regiment, the Durham Light Infantry, which was founded in 1758 and lasted right up until 1968. The horrors of First World War are shown, as is a reconstruction of a Durham street during the Second World War. Individual acts of bravery are also remembered, such as the story of Adam Wakenshaw, the youngest of a family of 13, who refused to leave his comrades after his arm was blown off. He died in action, and for this was

Market Place, Durham

awarded a Victoria Cross. The art gallery has a changing exhibition of paintings and sculpture.

A very different, but still outstanding, museum is the **Durham University Oriental Museum**, a collection of oriental art of international importance with material from Ancient Egypt, Tibet, India and China. The museum is located in parkland off Elvet Hill Road to the south of the city. The museum entrance is guarded by two stately Chinese lion-dogs.

The university also runs the 18-acre **Botanic Gardens**, on Hollingside Lane (off the A167) on the south side of the city. It is one of the newest in England, and has a large collection of North American trees, including junior-sized giant redwoods, a series of small "gardens-within-gardens" and walks through mature woodland. Two display greenhouses feature cacti and succulents

and a tropical "jungle". The gardens are closed between Christmas and New Year.

Crook Hall and Gardens is on Frankland Lane, a ten minute walk north of the Millburngate Shopping Centre. Centred on a lovely 14th century medieval manor house, the gardens have such features as the Secret Garden, the Shakespeare Garden, the Cathedral Garden and the Silver and White Gardens. The hall itself, with its haunted Jacobean Room, is open to the public.

AROUND DURHAM CITY

BRANCEPETH
4 miles SW of Durham on the A690

Brancepeth is a small estate village built by Matthew Russell in the early 19th century, with picturesque Georgian

THE ROYAL OAK

Commercial Street, Cornsay Colliery, Durham DH7 9BN
Tel: 0191 373 4224 Fax: 0191 373 4224

Cornsay Colliery can be found just three miles from Tow Law on the B6301 and in the heart of this small village you will find **The Royal Oak**. Dating back to 1871 this is a traditional country hostelry that is neatly presented and decked out with colourful window boxes and flowering tubs. The deceptively large interior has been lovingly refurbished and updated to ensure that customers old and new can enjoy the atmosphere at its best. The clientele is a good cross section of ages, attracting a strong local following as well as visitors to the area. The loyal support has been developed by the

husband and wife team that have owned and run The Royal Oak for over five years.

Behind the bar is stocked a good range of refreshing drinks, with a number of cask ales kept on tap, together with the usual leading brands of beer and lager. Food is also offered from a menu presenting classic English dishes that are freshly prepared and cooked to order. There is a games room, for whiling away a relaxing afternoon, and there is a beer garden to be enjoyed in warm weather. Live entertainment is also organised, with a regular Thursday night quiz and occasional karaoke and live music. Two letting rooms are planned to be available from Summer 2001.

cottages and an 18th century rectory. To the south, in parkland, is the imposing **Brancepeth Castle**. Seen from a distance, it looks suitably medieval and grand, but most of it dates from the same time as the building of the village. The original 13th century castle was owned by the Nevills, Earls of Westmorland.

Close to the castle is one of the saddest sights in County Durham - the remains of **St Brandon's Church**. In 1998 a fire destroyed everything but the four walls and tower of what was one of the county's most beautiful and historic buildings. The church's main glory, magnificent woodwork commissioned by its rector John Cosin in the early 17th century, was completely destroyed. Cosin went on to become Bishop of Durham, and restored many churches in the county.

Now an appeal is underway to restore the building, and work has already started.

FINCHALE PRIORY
4 miles N of Durham off the A167

On a minor road off the A167 lies 13th century **Finchale** (pronounced "Finkle") **Priory**. It was built by the monks of Durham Cathedral as a holiday retreat on the site of a hermitage founded by St Godric in about 1115. The ruins sit on a loop of the Wear in a beautiful location, across the river from **Cocken Wood Picnic Area**, which is linked to the priory by a bridge.

LANCHESTER
8 miles NW of Durham on the A691

Lanchester owes its name to the Roman fort of Longovicium ("The Long Fort"), which stood on a hilltop half a mile to the south-west. The fort was built to guard Dere Street, the Roman road

which linked York and the north. The scant remains sit on private land, however, and can't be visited. Stone from the fort was used in the mostly Norman **All Saints Church**, and Roman pillars can be seen supporting the north aisle. There is also a Roman altar in the south porch and some superb 12th century carvings over the vestry door in the chancel.

One place worth visiting near Lanchester is **Hall Hill Farm**, on the B6296 four miles south west of the village. It's a real working sheep farm which is open to the public all year round.

To the south of Lanchester is a typical County Durham mining area, with small colliery villages with names like **Quebec**, **Esh Winning**, **Tow Law** and **Cornsay Colliery**.

PITTINGTON
3 miles E of Durham off the B1283

A small village with one of County Durham's hidden gems - the Saxon-Norman **St Laurence's Church** at Hallgarth. It was partially rebuilt in the 19th century, though enough of the original fabric remains to make a visit well worth while. The 12th century paintings of St Cuthbert are well worth seeing.

BISHOP AUCKLAND

Bishop Auckland is an ancient town, standing on what was Dere Street, an old Roman road. Like many County Durham towns, it owed its later prosperity to coal mining. When the surrounding pits closed, the town went into decline, but it is now gradually rediscovering itself as new industries are established. As its name implies, up

QUEENS HEAD

Primrose Hill, Newfield,
Durham DL14 8BQ
Tel: 01388 606679

The small village of Newfield lies in the thinly populated area north of Bishop Auckland in the valley of the River Wear. **The Queens Head** lies in the heart of the village and caters mainly to the local community as well as to the occasional passer-by. The pub is bright and spacious with a great deal of character. A new beer garden has just been created and will be open in warm, dry weather for the enjoyment of all while in summer regular barbecues are planned. Inside there is ample seating so everyone can find a quiet corner in which to enjoy a drink or plenty of room for a large group of friends. To while away a long afternoon or evening there is also a games room with a pool table. If you are in need of a bite to eat then sandwiches, toasties and snacks are available all day on request.

Dating back to 1875 the Queens Head is a typical village pub enjoying a delightfully rural setting overlooking the river and the surrounding villages. The well-planned corner site is kept very neat in appearance and is located close to the village's new Millennium Green, known locally as The Shallies.

THE TRAVELLERS REST

7 Accrington Terrace, Evenwood, Durham DL14 9QD
Tel: 01388 8343822

The small village of Evenwood, not far from Bishop Auckland, has an industrial history going back 600 years as there was an ironworks here as early as the

14th century. Coal was discovered around 1384 and it was a mining village up until 1962 although now new

industry has replaced this as a form of employment. Today, Evenwood is a pleasant medium sized village with lots of green open spaces so if you are travelling through the area, then you could make a stop at the aptly named **Travellers Rest**. A small cosy pub, the interior is comfortable and welcoming with an open fire in the restaurant adding to the ambience.

If you are after a bite to eat then food is served Tuesday to Saturday evenings with a traditional roast lunch on Sunday. The meals are all freshly prepared and home cooked, using local produce, and there is a good selection to suit all tastes at reasonable prices. Entertainment is provided for locals and anyone else who would like to join in, with a quiz night each Tuesday and occasional line dancing classes in the function room upstairs. The room is also available for hire for private functions and parties. There is disabled access to the bar and restaurant.

until the first part of the 19th century, this was part of the territory of the Prince Bishops of Durham, who controlled what was then a scattering of small villages. Rapid expansion occurred during the 19th century and Bishop Auckland became an important market and administrative centre for the region.

Auckland Castle, still the official palace of the Bishop of Durham, began as a small 12th century manor house. It was added to by successive bishops, and looking at it today, you would imagine it was largely 17th or 18th century. But the fabric is still basically medieval, though parts of it were destroyed during the Civil War, when it was the the headquarters of Sir Arthur Hazlerigg, Governor of the North. Bishop Cosin set about making it wind and watertight after the Restoration, turning the Great Hall into a magnificent private chapel in 1665. Dedicated to St Peter, it is reputed

to be the largest private chapel in Europe.

The palace grounds, within which is a deer house, are open all year round, though the palace itself is only open from May until September.

A market has been held in Bishop Auckland for centuries. Opposite the present market place is the imposing Franco-Flemish **Bishop Auckland Town Hall**, built in the early 1860s.

Though the villages immediately surrounding Bishop Auckland are mainly industrial, there are still some attractions worth seeing. At South Church is the cathedralesque **St Andrew's Church**, 157 feet long and said to be the largest parish church in the county. And on display in a working men's club at West Auckland is an unusual trophy - the World Cup, no less.

In 1910 the village's football team

THE BRIDGE INN

1 Gordon Lane, Ramshaw, West Auckland, Durham DL14 0NS
Tel: 01388 832509 Fax: 01388 832509

The village of Ramshaw can be found just 4 miles west of Bishop Auckland and is located between the A68 and the A688, just a few minutes from the A1. This convenient location makes **The Bridge Inn** a popular stopping place for travellers and those exploring the area, as well as having a popular reputation with the locals. This is a fine, large roadside inn enjoying a prime site and is neatly presented with a brightly painted exterior that is well lit. Inside there is a comfortable, relaxing atmosphere that all the customers seem to enjoy. There is a separate 65-seater restaurant which serves an a la carte menu of top quality home cooked food and the windows of the restaurant look out over the marvellous surrounding countryside and a well equipped children's play area. Food can also be enjoyed in the bar areas with menus offering a wide choice of freshly prepared bar meals and snacks.

The Bridge Inn can offer overnight and short break accommodation with a total of seven rooms all with en-suite facilities, TV and hot drinks tray. The excellent guest facilities include a laundry, fax machine and photocopier with each of the bedrooms is individually designed and furnished, with a four poster room available for that special occasion. The surrounding area has much to offer the visitor with some delightful countryside, historic attractions and charming market towns to explore, making this an ideal base for a touring holiday.

headed off to Italy to represent England in the first ever "World Cup". It competed against teams from Germany, Italy and Switzerland, and surprisingly won the cup when it beat Juventus 2-0 in the final. The team returned the following year to defend their title, and again won the trophy, which they then retained for all time. But what you see is actually a replica, as the original was stolen.

Six miles to the east is Ferryhill, an ancient village that has been completely submerged in modern housing. The landscaping of the immense spoil heap from the quaintly named Dean and Chapter mine shows what progress has been made in the greening of the county's mining areas, as it is now an attractive, grassy hill.

THE UPLANDS HOTEL

Acacia Gardens, Crook,
County Durham DL15 9NB
Tel: 01388 762555 Fax: 01388 763555

The Uplands Hotel can be found just off the B6298, just half a mile from Crook on the A689. The property was built just prior to World War One as a private residence and remained so until 1947 when it became a hotel. The property has recently been taken over by new owners and has been extensively refurbished with the whole interior having been updated to create a fresh luxurious feel throughout. When you walk in for the first time you have the impression of

AROUND BISHOP AUCKLAND

BINCHESTER
1 mile N of Bishop Auckland off the A689

Binchester Roman Fort was known to the Romans as Vinovia, and was built about AD80. It was one of a chain of forts built along Dere Street, and has the best preserved Roman military bathhouse in Britain, complete with pillared hypocaust. As well as acting as a military centre controlling the local area, the fort also provided a stopping-off place for troops and supplies heading towards Hadrian's Wall. A portion of the actual Dere Street itself has been preserved here.

entering an exclusive, private club, yet the atmosphere is warm and welcoming.

Here you can find high quality accommodation, enjoy a delicious meal in the restaurant, have a drink or enjoy a bar meal with friends in one of the two bars. Ideally located for a touring holiday in the area, The Uplands offers five bedrooms, all en-suite, with colour TV and hot drinks facilities. Food and drinks are served throughout the day in the Lounge and pub bars, with a good selection of well-kept ales, draught lagers and some excellent stouts. The stylish and intimate restaurant seats up to 50 and the menu is put together by the top class chefs and presents freshly prepared dishes using the finest local ingredients. To complement your meal, the hotel offers a fine, international wine list.

CROOK
5 miles NW of Bishop Auckland on the A689

Crook is a small, spacious, town with a wide square, which, in summer, is full of flowers. At one time it was a centre of coal mining, and the quaintly named Billy Row to the north of the town centre is a typical coalfield hamlet of miners' cottages.

ESCOMB
2 miles NW of Bishop Auckland off the A688

In the small village of Escomb is one of the true hidden gems of County Durham - **St John the Evangelist Church**, built using stone from nearby Binchester Roman Fort. This is one of only three complete Saxon churches in Britain, and is typically Saxon in layout, with its long, high nave and tiny chancel arch, which may have been taken from the Roman fort at Binchester. In the south wall of the nave is a curious sundial surrounded by serpents and surmounted by what may be a mythical beast.

SHILDON
2 miles SE of Bishop Auckland on the B6282

Timothy Hackworth was, from 1825, the resident engineer on the Stockton to Darlington Railway. In 1840 he resigned to develop the Soho Engine Works at Shildon, and make his own locomotives. Now these works, plus his house, form **The Timothy Hackworth Victorian Railway Museum** (see panel on page 14).

STAINDROP
7 miles SW of Bishop Auckland on the A688

Staindrop is a delightful, very typical, Durham village, linear in form and with a long village green lined with Georgian houses. **St Mary's Church** has a Saxon core, and inside are the tombs of the two great families who have owned **Raby Castle** on the outskirts of the village - the Nevills and the Vanes.

Raby is County Durham's largest medieval castle, in a magnificent setting of parkland - a romantic, fairy-tale building which was the home of the Nevill family, who were powerful northern barons. In the 16th century in

St Mary's Church, Staindrop

the great Baron's Hall, over 700 barons assembled to plot the overthrow of Elizabeth 1. For this, the castle and all the Nevill estates were seized by the Crown. It was later leased to Sir Henry Vane, James 1's Secretary of State. Much of the interior is now Georgian and Victorian, though the Great Kitchen remains virtually unaltered after 600 years.

TIMOTHY HACKWORTH VICTORIAN & RAILWAY MUSEUM

Hackworth Close, Shildon, County Durham DL4 1PQ
Tel/Fax: 01388 777999 Website: www.hackworthmsueum.co.uk

County Durham is famous as being the birthplace of the railways, thanks to the famous Stockton to Darlington railway. Timothy Hackworth was, from 1825, the superintendent engineer on the line, and in 1840, realising the huge potential of rail travel, he resigned to develop the famous Soho Engine

works at Shildon, and make his own locomotives. It was here that the first trains to run in Russia and Nova Scotia were built, and many ships were powered by marine engines designed and built on the premises.

Now the whole 15 acre complex, plus his house, form nucleus for the **Timothy Hackworth Victorian & Railway Museum**, which gives a fascinating insight into the early days of rail and steam power in England. Timothy was a true son of the North East, having been born at Wylam-on-Tyne in Northumberland in 1786, and dying in 1850 in the house

that now forms part of the museum. He was a born engineer, and one of his earliest machines was the famous "Puffing Billy". He later worked for George Stephenson at his works in Newcastle before moving to the Stockton to Darlington Railway.

Thanks to him, Shildon became the first railway town in the world. Now it attracts thousands of tourists each year who want to find out about the transport revolution that took place in the early 1800s. The Soho engine shed dates back to the 1820s, and houses a Hackworth beam engine (which can operate at the press of a button), the locomotive

"Braddyll" (standing on the exact spot where it may have been painted 160 years ago), an 1850s coal wagon and an 1860s passenger coach from the Stockton to Darlington railway. Perhaps one of the most interesting exhibits in the museum is a full sized replica of the "Sans Pareil", a locomotive Timothy built for the Rainhill Trials of 1829 on the Liverpool to Manchester railway. There's also a working rail line from the museum's good's shed to the coal drops at Shildon Station. Visitors can sometimes take trips on the line, being pulled by the locomotive "Merlin". Timothy Hackworth's house has period rooms, models, a marvellous audio visual display and some smaller exhibits.

You don't need to be a railway buff to enjoy the Timothy Hackworth Museum. It has plenty of hands-on and interactive exhibits, and won the "Pride of Northumbria" award in 1999 for being the best visitor attraction of the year in the under 100,000 visitor category. Opening Times: Wednesday to Sunday from Good Friday until last Sunday in October 10.00-17.00 daily; Admission charge

Raby Castle, nr Staindrop

about the social and industrial life of the valley.

WITTON-LE-WEAR
4 miles NW of Bishop Auckland off the A68

Overlooking the River Wear is Witton-le-Wear, a village with terraces down the hillside, notable for its handsome green, its open views, attractive cottages and a pele tower attached to fragments of a medieval manor house in the High Street. The grounds of **Witton Castle**, a medieval fortified house just across the river, are now open to the public and, as well as walks through the parkland, there are

Four miles north of Staindrop is Butterknowle, with, close by, the **Gaunless Valley Visitor Centre**, housed in what was the Stag's Head Inn. Here visitors can see displays and exhibits

THE ROYAL OAK

Staindrop, Darlington, Durham
Tel: 01833 660281

On the main street of the attractive village of Staindrop, close to Raby castle, visitors will find **The Royal Oak** public house, located in a terrace of houses, adjacent to St Mary's Church. Built in the 16th century the property has stood the test of time, having catered to the refreshment requirements of the villagers for over 400 years. Inside you can choose between the cosy public bar with a roaring open fire at cooler times of year, or the lounge bar, which features some very attractive sporting dog prints and is decorated with interesting bric-a-brac. There is a very cosy dining room but you can also eat in the bars. An excellent variety of foods are offered from the menu with the addition of "specials" and choices of traditional Sunday lunches are excellent value. All dishes are freshly prepared and home-cooked. The bar stocks a wide range of ales including cask and a choice of draught lagers.

Traditional entertainment is provided with a pool room and darts area, while a more modern addition to the public bar, is the satellite TV on which major live sporting events can be seen. There is also a regular Sunday night pub quiz and occasionally entertainment is arranged.

THE VICTORIA INN

School Street, Witton-le-Wear,
Bishop Auckland, County Durham DL14 0AS
Tel: 01388 488501 Fax: 01388 488827

At the heart of the village of Witton-le-Wear, just off the A68, stands **The Victoria Inn**. This traditional country inn and restaurant dates back to the 17th century and is a fine example of rural hospitality at its best.

This is very much a food oriented pub with the quality being of a very high standard, freshly prepared to order using locally-sourced produce by the resident chef. The varied menu offers an excellent range of home cooked dishes catering to all tastes and appetites, ranging from light starters and snacks through to a fine selection of main dishes. There is an equally tempting selection of desserts with which to round off your meal. Here you can certainly enjoy a delicious three-course meal prepared to the highest of standards, and without breaking the bank either! Food is served each lunch time and evening, and advance booking is highly recommended at weekends to avoid disappointment.

There is a friendly and relaxed atmosphere and a warm welcome is extended to regular visitors and new faces. If you are after a refreshing drink then the bar stocks a selection of cask ales and there is plenty of seating to allow you to find a quiet corner in which to enjoy it. Entertainment is provided with quiz nights being Thursday and Sunday. This is a convenient stopping place if you are travelling through, or touring the area.

swimming and paddling pools, refreshments, fishing, a games room, and a shop.

DARLINGTON

Darlington, just off the A1(M). is an important regional centre serving the southern part of County Durham, Teesdale and much of North Yorkshire. It was founded in Saxon times, and has a bustling town centre with one of the largest market places in England. On its west side is the Old Town Hall and indoor market, with an imposing **Clock Tower**, designed by the famous Victorian Alfred Waterhouse in 1864, lording over it all, and on the south side is the Dolphin Leisure Centre, opened in 1983.

There are many fine buildings to be enjoyed in Darlington, perhaps most notably **St Cuthbert's Church** on the east side of the market place, with its tall spire. It is almost cathedral-like in its proportions, and was built by Bishop Pudsey between 1183 and 1230 as a collegiate church. Its slender lancet windows and steep roof enhance its beauty, which has earned it the name "The Lady of the North".

Perhaps Darlington's greatest claim to fame lies in the role it played with its neighbour Stockton in the creation of the world's first commercially successful public railway which opened in 1825. It was the Darlington Quaker and banker Edward Pease who became the main driving force behind the railway scheme to link the Durham coalfield with the port of Stockton.

The present Darlington Station at Bank Top came from a much later period in the railway age, as lines were being constructed to link England and

Stephenson's Locomotion No 1, Darlington

pioneering Stockton and Darlington Railway. This includes a replica of Stephenson's **Locomotion No 1**, a Stockton and Darlington first class coach carriage built in 1846, "Little Giant", (a 15 inch gauge miniature locomotive), a World War 11 newsstand, the **Derwent**, (the earliest surviving Darlington-built locomotive), a model of the Stockton to Darlington railway, and even Victorian urinals.

Scotland. The original Darlington Station, built in 1842, was located at North Road Station. Today it is the **Darlington Railway Centre and Museum**, a museum of national importance which houses relics of the

So much early railway history is to be seen in this part of County Durham that British Rail have named their local Bishop Auckland-Darlington-Middlesbrough line the **Heritage Line**.

THE COUNTRYMAN

Dunwell Lane, Bolam, Nr. Darlington, County Durham DL2 2UP
Tel: 01388 834577 Fax: 01388 834577

In the small village of Bolam, just off the B6275, you will find **The Countryman Inn**. This is a large, popular establishment enjoying a large site surrounded by grounds extending to three acres. Although this is a very rural location, with no sizeable towns nearby, it maintains a loyal local clientele drawn here by the quality of food and drink on offer. The bar stocks Black Sheep cask ale with a wide range of guest beers from other local breweries. The standard of the ale on offer has gone some way to account for The Countryman being the Darlington CAMRA 'Country Pub of Year 2000' award winner.

The quality of food is of an equally exceptional standard with the dishes being freshly prepared to order by a chef. The style of the food on offer is described as 'fusion cooking' with an eclectic mix of eastern and western cuisine. The specialities are the home-made ice-cream and breads which are prepared by the chef on the premises. The stylish restaurant area can seat 80 and the tables are well presented with linen table cloths and candles. Booking is advisable at weekends. Live entertainment is provided with occasional karaoke, folk and jazz nights.

Darlington Railway Museum

foot of Post House Wynd, is a life-size floral replica of Locomotion No 1.

High Row, with its elevated street of shops makes an impressive sight, and forms part of a compact but characterful shopping centre. The tall buildings evolved because of the narrowness of the plots of land in medieval times. The façades are pierced by tunnels which at one time gave access to rear gardens. These have long since been built over as yards and lend their name to this part of town. The "yards" now contain shops and small businesses and are public rights of way between High Row and Skinnergate.

To continue the railways theme, there's an unusual engine to be seen in Morton Park - it's a full size model made of bricks, and was designed by sculptor David Mach. And above High Row at the

THE BAY HORSE

Hurworth, Nr. Darlington,
Durham DL2 2AA
Tel: 01325 720663
Fax: 01325 722437

The village of Hurworth can be found just a few miles from Darlington and here visitors will find the delightful **Bay Horse** public house enjoying a superb central location in this picturesque village.

This is a large, sprawling pub with an ornate frontage, dating back to the 15th century when it was originally a coaching inn. Inside you will find a large, spacious interior with a well-furnished lounge and bar together with a beautiful conservatory restaurant area.

Food is served each lunch-time and evening, seven days a week. The menu offers a wide choice of English, Continental and Asian dishes catering to all tastes and appetites. Vegetarians and children are also well provided for. The meals are well priced and each one is freshly prepared to order. The bar stocks a good range of beer and lager with many leading brands featured. The owner, Mike Henderson, is a local man and in the two years he has been here, has built up a good reputation for serving fine food and drink with friendly, amiable staff. Mike, together with his wife Margaret, is also responsible for organising the weekly Tuesday quiz night, so if you fancy pitting your wits against the locals then why not call in.

AROUND DARLINGTON

GAINFORD

7 miles W of Darlington on the A67

Gainford is considered to be County Durham's most beautiful village - surely one of its hidden places. It sits just north of the Tees, and its core is a jostling collection of 18th and 19th century cottages and houses grouped round a green, each one quaint and picturesque.

At the SW corner of the green is the building that draws everything together - **St Mary's Church**. It's a large church, built mostly in the 12th century, from, it is believed, stones from Piercebridge Roman fort, three miles to the east. Certainly a Roman altar was found built into the tower during the restoration of 1864-65, and it can be seen in the museum of Durham Cathedral.

Gainford Hall is a large Jacobean mansion built by the Rev. John Cradock in the early 1600s. Though not open to the public, it can be viewed from the road. It's hard to believe that in the 19th century this quiet village was a spa, visited by people from all over the north of England. Some way away along the banks of the Tees to the west a basin can be seen where the sulphurous waters were collected.

HEIGHINGTON

5 miles N of Darlington off the A6072

An attractive village with neat cottages and a large green. **St Michael's Church** is mainly Norman, and has a pre-Reformation oak pulpit with prayers inscribed on it for its donors, Alexander and Agnes Fletcher. About three miles west of the village, near Bolam, is the shaft of a 9th century cross known as the **Legs Cross**.

THE DOG INN

Cross Lane End, Heighington, Nr. Darlington, Durham DL2 2TX
Tel: 01325 312152

The Dog Inn can be found just five miles from Darlington travelling North along the A68. Enjoying a prime corner location, visitors will find the delightful **Dog Inn** on the A68. The charming stone building dates from the late 19th century when it was built as a hostelry to serve the local community. The Dog has a very inviting appeal and as visitors walk through the door for the first they will quickly become aware of how friendly and welcoming an establishment it is. The interior is well designed ensuring that you can always find a quiet corner for an intimate drink while also allowing plenty of room for small groups to gather. The decor retains many of the original features of the building with well worn wood floors and low beamed ceilings.

Here you can enjoy some delicious food that has been freshly prepared in the pub's kitchens. The menu offers an excellent choice of traditional dishes catering to varied tastes and all appetites. The bar stocks a range of beers and lager with a regularly changing guest cask ale also available. If you are in need of accommodation then you need look no further, as the Dog is also able to provide bed and breakfast. There is one single and two twin rooms, all with an en-suite bathroom, colour TV and hot drinks tray.

CARLBURY ARMS

Piercebridge, Nr. Darlington,
County Durham DL2 3SJ
Tel: 01325 374286

The Carlbury Arms is an outstanding public house and restaurant found just off the main A67, five miles west of Darlington. The premises date back to the 17th century, as reflected in the original stone floors, exposed beams, sandstone walls and other features that have been retained throughout. Once known as The Wheatsheaf, it was given the name of the Carlbury Arms by the current owners Richard and Barbara, who named it after a village was once located here and of which only one house now remains. Richard and Barbara have been in residence since 1998; Barbara is the chef while Richard looks after front of house and together with their capable and friendly staff they offer all customers a warm welcome and genuine hospitality.

Completely refurbished and redesigned, the interior of this charming pub is beautiful and welcoming, with many handsome furnishings and tasteful decor throughout. Open all day every day, food is served at lunchtime and evenings with the cosy and intimate restaurant (non smoking) seating 20. Meals can also be taken in the main bar areas. Booking is advised Wednesday - Saturday evenings and Sunday lunch. The range of excellent food on offer includes traditional favourites such as home-made steak and kidney pie, gammon, chicken dishes, fresh fish and vegetarian choices. There is a fine selection of daily lunchtime and evening specials and guests should be sure to leave room for one of the tempting desserts. Well-kept ales include John Smiths, Theakston's, Black Sheep and guest ales, along with a good complement of stout, draught lager, cider, wine and spirits.

THE CROSSHILL HOTEL

1/2 The Square, Sedgefield,
County Durham TS21 2AB
Tel: 01740 620153 Fax: 01740 621206

Enjoying one of the best locations within the heart of the village of Sedgefield, right on the village green, is **The Crosshill Hotel**. This fine listed building has an impressive frontage which has stood the test of time well, considering it was originally built as a coaching inn over 300 years ago. The three story building conceals a delightful, country style interior with many splendid features. The hotel can offer six comfortable en-suite rooms available throughout the year. The rooms vary in size and are provided with TV and hot drinks tray and boast a tourist board three star grading. The Crosshill Restaurant provides a stylish setting in which to savour the delicious offerings of the menu. The cuisine ranges from Oriental and Thai to Mexican and Caribbean, with plenty of choice to tempt every palate. Traditional Northumbrian dishes also feature with fresh local produce used wherever possible.

Within the same building, visitors will also find The Inn on the Green, owned and run by the same couple, Tracy and Darren Gouldburn. The couple have recently refurbished both the public and lounge bars and these are a cosy place in which to relax and enjoy a drink. Darren is the chef responsible for both the Crosshill Restaurant and the food served within The Inn on the Green, and the menu on offer here displays an equally international selection. The pub, hotel and restaurant are developing a good reputation for providing good food and quality accommodation, and are also well placed for travellers exploring the area. Well worth making a detour for.

LOW DINSDALE
4 miles SE of Darlington off the A67

A visit on foot or by car to Low Dinsdale is well worthwhile, as the 12th century red sandstone **St John the Baptist Church** surrounded by copper beaches is worthy of a postcard. Opposite stands a 16th century manor house built on the site of a moated Norman manor owned by the Siward family. They later changed their name to Surtees, and became well known throughout the north.

MIDDLETON ST GEORGE
3 miles E of Darlington off the A67

Middleton St George is a pleasant village on the banks of the River Tees to the

River Tees, Middleton-One-Row

east of Darlington, near Teesside International Airport, once an airfield from which British and Canadian bombers flew during World War II. **St George's Church** dates from the 13th century with 18th and 19th century additions, and is detached from the village, standing among fields. Curiously, the stonework has been heavily patched with brick at some point. It is thought to have been built on the site of an old Saxon church and the Victorian pews are rather

incongruous - rather more like old fashioned waiting room seats than pews.

The nearby village of **Middleton One Row** is aptly named - consisting only of a row of Georgian cottages. The cottages have inevitably been altered over the years and the arrival of the railway inspired some growth.

PIERCEBRIDGE
4Ω miles W of Darlington on the A67

Driving past the picturesque village green of Piercebridge, most motorists will be unaware that they are passing through the centre of a once important Roman fort. This was one of a chain of forts on Dere street, which linked the northern Roman headquarters at York with the north. Other forts in the chain were at Catterick to the south and Binchester, just outside Bishop Auckland, to the north. The remains of the fort, which are visible today, can be dated from coin evidence to around AD270. The site is always open and admission is free. Finds from this site are housed in the Bowes Museum at Barnard Castle.

SEDGEFIELD
9 miles NE of Darlington on the A689

Sedgefield, famous nowadays for its race course, is a small town whose market charter was issued in 1315. The bulky 15th century tower of **St Edmund's Church** dominates the green, and the cluster of Georgian and early Victorian houses. It is famous for its intricately carved Cosin woodwork, which was on a par with the woodwork lost when Brancepeth church was destroyed by fire in 1998. Cosin's son-in-law, Denis

Granville, was rector here in the late 17th century, and it was at this time that the woodwork was installed.

Hardwick Hall Country Park, owned by Durham County Council, lies to the west of the town, beyond the A177. Within the 40-acre park is a lake, a Gothic folly, and a network of woodland walks. The original parkland was laid out in the 18th century by the architect James Paine.

STOCKTON-ON-TEES
9 miles E of Darlington on the A166

Stockton-on-Tees is famous for being one end of the Stockton to Darlington railway, opened in 1825 so that coal from the mines of South Durham could have access to the Tees, where it would be shipped south to London.

Nowadays it's a large, busy town, and not part of County Durham any more. When local government reorganisation created the county of Cleveland, Stockton found itself on the wrong side of the border, and when Cleveland itself was dissolved, the town became a unitary authority, taking in parts of what used to be North Yorkshire.

John Walker, the inventor of the humble friction match, was born here in 1781, and Thomas Sheraton, the furniture maker and designer, was born here in 1751, though he eventually moved to London. One unusual citizen of the town was Ivy Close, who won Britain's first ever beauty contest in 1908

Preston Hall Museum, in 110 acres of parkland to the south of the town on the banks of the Tees, is housed in what was the home of a local shipbuilder, Robert Ropner. Now it is has exhibits explaining how life was lived in the area since Preston Hall was built in 1825. There's a fully furnished drawing room

of the 1820s, plus a typical bedsit of the 1960s. In the cellars there's a collection of arms and armour.

In the centre of Stockton's High Street is the Old Town Hall and market cross dating from the mid 18th century, and in Theatre Yard off the High Street is the **Green Dragon Museum**, set in a former sweet factory warehouse. Here the visitor can explore Stockton's history and people, plus gaze at what is possibly the most unusual object in any North East museum - skiffle king Lonnie Donegan's hair brush.

The parish church, in red brick, was built between 1712 and 1713, and is one of only a handful of Anglican churches in England without a dedication. It's official title is **The Parish Church of Stockton-on-Tees**, though for many years it has been informally called "St Thomas's". This unofficial dedication came from a chapel of ease that stood on the site when Stockton was a part of the parish of Norton.

Stockton was once a busy port, but this is no more. There is now a lot of development along the banks of the Tees, due to the **Tees Barrage** downstream of the town. This was built to stop the flow of pollution from the chemical plants being carried upstream by the tides. Now the river is no longer tidal at Stockton and for 15 miles inland, and can be used for a variety of recreational purposes. The barrage has a navigation lock, a large canoe slalom and a fish pass.

The **Teesside Princess** is a river cruiser which takes visitors on a pleasure trip as far inland as Yarm, stopping at Preston Hall. It sails daily, except on Mondays, from the Castlegate Quay. Moored at the quay is a replica of Captain Cook's famous ship, **Endeavour**. Due to the clean up in water quality, there is also a water sports centre. The **Millennium Bridge**, linking Stockton and the opposite bank of the Tees, opened in 2000.

HARTLEPOOL

There are really two Hartlepools - the old town on the headland, and the newer part, which used to be called West Hartlepool. Up until 1968 they were separate boroughs, but they have now combined under the one name. This town, like Stockton-on-Tees and Darlington, is a unitary authority, though the border with County Durham is almost on its outskirts.

The old part of Hartlepool goes back centuries, and was at one time a walled town. Parts of these walls still exist on the shore line, and there is a particularly fine gatehouse, called the **Sandwellgate**, with solid turrets in either side. Go through the pointed archway, and you find yourself on the beach.

In the Middle Ages, Hartlepool was the only port within County Durham that was allowed to trade outside the Palatinate, which made it an important place. After the Norman Conquest, it was acquired by the Bruce family, whose most notable member was Robert the Bruce, King of Scotland. It received its charter about 1201 from King John, who ordered that the walls to be built to defend it against the marauding Scots.

The immense and ornate 13th century **St Hilda's Church** was built by the Bruces as a burial place, which may explain its size. Within is the tomb of what is thought to be Robert Bruce, the church's founder. It sits behind the altar, and is made of Frosterley marble.

The church stands on the site of a monastery founded by St Aidan in AD647. Its most famous abbess was Hilda - hence the church's dedication - who subsequently went on to found the great monastery at Whitby, where the Synod of Whitby was held in AD664. Parts of its cemetery were excavated in the 19th century, and some of the finds are on show in Durham and Newcastle.

Hartlepool's harbour eventually went into decline, and by the early 18th century the place was no more than a fishing village. In 1835 work started on opening up the harbour once more, and rail links were established with the coalfields. But it had competition. In 1847 work started on the West Harbour and Coal Dock, and by 1860 it was thriving. Other docks were opened, and soon a new town grew up around them. So West Hartlepool was born. On December 16 1914 it was the first town in Britain to suffer from enemy action during the First World War when it was shelled from German warships lying off the coast.

Nowadays it is a thriving shopping centre, with some outstanding tourist attractions, including the **Hartlepool Historic Quay and Museum**. A small seaport has been constructed round one of the old docks, showing what life was like in the early part of the 19th century, when Britain was at war with France. Grouped round the small dock are various businesses and shops, such as a printer, gunsmith, naval tailor, swordsmith and instrument maker. Visitors can also go aboard **HMS Trincomalee**, Britain's oldest surviving warship (launched in 1817), and have coffee aboard the **PSS Wingfield Castle**, an old paddle steamer. The Trincomalee, strictly speaking, is a separate attraction, so there is an extra charge.

Attached is the Hartlepool Museum, with exhibits showing life in the town

THE BLUE BELLS

Newton Bewley, Nr. Wolviston,
Billingham, Cleveland TS22 5PQ
Tel: 01740 644498
Fax: 01748 644498
website www.thebluebell.co.uk

Just off the A689, to the north of Billingham, is the small village of Newton Bewley. Here is the delightful Victorian establishment of **The Blue Bells**, enjoying a prime position easily located by visitors entering the village. Originally built in 1842 the property has in recent years been refurbished and updated to provide a neat appearance to today's customers. The first thing you will see as you approach is the extensive car park and large children's play area, ideal for occupying younger family members. The interior has been well planned with plenty of space and yet also with smaller areas which can feel more intimate. There is a bar and lounge furnished with wooden chairs, stools and copper topped tables while the lovely restaurant is also well thought out. The whole place is spotlessly clean and the atmosphere is friendly and welcoming.

Regular visitors are attracted by the quality and variety of food on offer and the varied menus are changed regularly to make the most of seasonal produce and to enable the chef to display his culinary flair. The selection of dishes available includes classic English dishes together with some more interesting and unusual options. Recently under new management, visit the website for up to date news and developments.

THE McCORVILLE INN

The Green, Elwick, Hartlepool,
Cleveland TS27 3EF
Tel: 01429 273344

The village of Elwick is just on the Cleveland side of the Durham border, just off the A19, and is a surprising find in this little known corner of England. This pretty picture postcard village features a number of attractive little cottages while old stone walls line the narrow lanes. Enjoying a classic spot, overlooking the village green, is the equally charming **McCorville Inn**. Taking its name from a famous race horse, the late 19th century building is neatly presented with a white painted front and black painted window frames and doors.

The interior is equally delightful, furnished throughout with an array of small tables, chairs and stools. There is an open fire that adds to the ambience in cooler months while the walls are decorated with collections of prints and bone china. The McCorville Arms is popular with the locals both for its beer and the food, which is available each lunchtime. The menu offers a selection of simple, classic bar meals and snacks, freshly prepared and reasonably priced. Pensioners and children can enjoy smaller meals that are offered at even better value. Vegetarians are well catered for. Families welcome. The traditional Sunday lunches are very popular so you are advised to arrive early to be sure of a table.

through the ages. It features "sea monsters", a medieval "round house", and interactive displays.

Close by is **Jackson's Landing**, a new shopping mall next to a recently opened marina whilst in the former Christ Church is **Hartlepool Art Gallery**. The local tourism information office is here as well, and the visitor can climb the church tower for a view over the town.

AROUND HARTLEPOOL

BILLINGHAM
5 miles SW of Hartlepool, off the A19

Modern Billingham came about because of the great chemical plants that surrounded the River Tees. But though the town looks modern, it is in fact an ancient place, possibly founded by Bishop Ecgred of Lindisfarne in the 9th century. **St Cuthbert's Church** has a 10th century Saxon tower, and Saxon walls survive in the nave. The chancel was rebuilt and widened in 1939 to provide for the town's growing population due to the influx of workers to the chemical plants. Close by is the attractive village of **Wolviston**.

Captain Cook Monument, Billingham

ELWICK
4 miles W of Hartlepool off the A19

Elwick is a small, pretty village with patches of village green running up each side of a main street lined with neat, unassuming cottages. **St Peter's Church** has a nave dating from the 13th century. The chancel was rebuilt in the 17th century, using materials from the previous chancel, and its tower was added on in 1813. On either side of the chancel arch are two small Saxon carvings - possibly fragments of grave markers.

GREATHAM
3 miles S of Hartlepool of the A689

Close to Greatham stands **Hartlepool Nuclear Power Station**. English Nature, the power station, Hartlepool Council and the Teesmouth Field Centre have come together to protect and enhance the marshes, tidal flats and dunes on the north shore of the Tees estuary. It's now a protected area, and popular with people who come to view its large seal population.

HART
2 miles NW of Hartlepool on the A179

In this quiet village stands the mother church of Hartlepool - **St Mary Magdalene's Church**. It shows examples of architecture from all medieval periods, and even before. The nave is Saxon, the tower and font are Norman, and the chancel is early 19th century.

On the outer wall of the White Hart Inn is a figurehead, said to have

THE MANOR HOUSE HOTEL

Market Street, Ferryhill, Durham DL17 8JH
Tel: 01740 654322 Fax: 01740 656735
e-mail info@ferryhillmanorhouse.co.uk
website www.ferryhillmanorhouse.co.uk

The Manor House is a small family run hotel,
licensed restaurant and public bar which can be
found in the heart of the town of Ferryhill, opposite
the town hall. The Manor House has a long history
dating back to the 16th century when it was
probably built as a Yeoman farmer's dwelling. Over
the years the property changed hands many times
until it eventually passed into the ownership of John Thomas in 1997. He has since carefully restored
and modernised the hotel while retaining its traditional character and charm.

The interior features the original wooden floors, exposed beams, open brickwork and real fires all
adding to the atmosphere of the place. Visitors can enjoy simply
a quiet drink in the bar, or a snack or meal chosen from the
impressive menu. Entertainment is provided with quiz nights
each Monday and Thursday together with live music most
weekends. The restaurant provides both smoking and non-
smoking areas and offers an excellent choice of dishes from
full a la carte and table d'hote menus. All meals are prepared
by the top class chefs and utilise fresh local produce wherever
possible. The accommodation comprises 8 top quality bedrooms
of varying sizes. All are en-suite and superbly furnished to
provide comfortable accommodation to satisfy the most
exacting of tastes.

THE BIRD IN HAND

Salters Lane, Trimdon Village,
County Durham TS29 6JQ
Tel: 01429 880391 Fax: 01429 882010

Trimdon Village is one of a few
'Trimdons' that can be found just a few
miles north of Sedgefield. This particular
village was, like much of this area, a
mining village though its recorded
history goes back much further. It was
once a medieval settlement and St
Mary's Church, located on a low mound
in the centre of the village, is Norman.

The Bird in Hand public house is a
much more recent addition to the
village, having been built in 1955. It has a delightful conservatory frontage, which appears very
inviting, and the whole building is tastefully painted. The building also enjoys an elevated position
with some fine views over the surrounding countryside. Inside there is a cosy public bar which is
always busy with customers from the surrounding area. There is also a games room, with a pool table
and darts board, a good sized lounge and a large conservatory restaurant. The bar stocks a selection of
cask ales with regular guest beers. Food is served each day at lunch time and in the evening with a
menu offering a good range of simple, tasty bar food with something to suit all tastes. The house
speciality of Steak and Black Sheep Ale pie is to be highly recommended. A traditional Sunday lunch
is served and, unusually, The Bird in Hand opens for breakfast each morning from 10.00 a.m. Live
entertainment is provided for the enjoyment of all customers in the form of live music each Friday
and a pub quiz each Sunday. Other facilities include a large car park and beer garden.

been a relic from the "Rising Sun", which was shipwrecked off Hartlepool in 1861

PETERLEE
6 miles N of Hartlepool off the A19

Peterlee is a new town which was established in 1948 to rehouse the mining families which lived in the colliery villages around Easington and Shotton. It was named in honour of an outstanding Durham miner and county councillor, Peter Lee, who fought all his life for the well-being of the local community. The town has a modern shopping centre, a tourist information office and a market. Close by is the village of **Easington**, whose fine old **St Mary's Church** sits on a low hill. The tower is Norman, and within is some Cosin-style woodwork.

Castle Eden Dene National Nature Reserve, on the south side of the town, is of national importance, being one of the largest woodlands in the northeast which has not been planted or extensively altered by man. It covers 500 acres and lies in a steep-sided valley on magnesian limestone, with a wide variety of native trees and shrubs, wild flowers, bird life and butterflies, including the Castle Eden Argus, which is found only in eastern County Durham. There is a network of footpaths, some steep and narrow; visitors are requested to keep to paths at all times to avoid damage. The site is managed by English Nature and it makes sense to begin a visit at the Reserve Centre, Oakerside Dene Lodge, Stanhope Chase, Peterlee, where leaflets and information are available.

TRIMDON
9 miles W of Hartlepool on the B1278

There is a trio of villages with the word "Trimdon" in their name - Trimdon Grange, Trimdon Colliery and Trimdon itself. It's a quiet village with a wide main street and the unpretentious medieval **St Mary Magdalene's Church**.

Trimdon Colliery is two miles to the NE, and it was here, in 1882, that the Trimdon Colliery pit disaster took place. A great underground explosion claimed the lives of 74 miners.

2 Northern County Durham

The area south of the Tyne is largely industrial in character, encompassing large towns and cities in Tyne and Wear such as Gateshead, Sunderland and South Shields and, further out in County Durham, smaller towns like Chester-le-Street and Consett. But there is still plenty to see, especially in Gateshead and Sunderland, which, like many large British conurbations, are re-discovering themselves and their heritage. And open space and country-side, especially to the south, are still there to be explored as well.

Metro Centre, Gateshead

Up until the mid 70s, this used to be County Durham, with a small portion to the west in Northumberland. But local government reorganisation placed most of it in Tyne and Wear, which itself has disappeared as an administrative county. Old allegiances remain, however, and like Hartlepool and Stockton-on-Tees to the south, some of the people in the area look upon themselves as Durhamites.

Gateshead lies immediately south of Newcastle-upon-Tyne, on the banks of the River Tyne. It has always retained its own peculiar identity however, and owes

Gibside Estate

little to its big brother immediately to the north, no matter how much cooperation has taken place over the years. It is now redeveloping its riverside area, with such attractions as the Gateshead Millennium Bridge and the Music Centre. Gateshead also has the Metro Centre, one of Britain's largest shopping centres.

To the east, South Shields is an area that has, in that peculiar British way, become associated with a famous writer. For the town is now Catherine Cookson Country, with a Catherine Cookson Trail and a Catherine Cookson

North of England Open Air Museum

Exhibition in the local museum. And Jarrow has its Venerable Bede associations, and a church that partly goes back to the great man's time.

Sunderland, to the south, also has Bede associations. This is one of England's newer cities, and it has the first minster to be created in England since the Reformation.

But Sunderland is under-going a reform-ation of its own. No longer can it be dis-missed as an industrial town, with not much to see or do. It has a fully refurbished winter gardens, museum and art gallery, and the National Glass Centre. It will soon also be linked up to Tyneside's own underground rail system, the Metro Rapid Transport System.

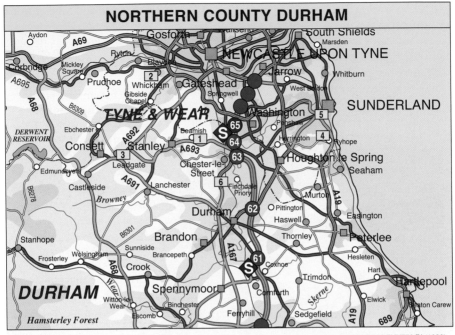

© MAPS IN MINUTES ™ (1999)

PLACES TO STAY, EAT, DRINK AND SHOP

GATESHEAD

Gateshead has perhaps suffered from its proximity to its big sister, Newcastle, for generations. Thanks to the **Metro Centre**, an impressive shopping and leisure complex, the borough is very much on the map as a place where

Metro Centre, Gateshead

Tynesiders and many other people go - not just to shop, but for entertainment in various forms.

The Metro Centre is really what Gateshead is most famous for. It is easy to fin-Borough of Gateshead and has achieved some notable successes in the "Britain in Bloom" competitions. The eight glasshouses, covering 3,034 square metres, have computer-controlled heating systems. Every year the nurseries host a major spring and summer flower show. An important part of the service offered is plant information for the

general public. This is based in the showhouse which has pools, fish and ornamental planting. Visitors can enjoy the herb garden, rose garden, heather and conifer garden and tree and shrub nursery. There is also a picnic area.

But Gateshead is a town that is looking to the future, and there are some exciting new projects that should revitalise the area. Next to the A1 on Gateshead's southern approaches is one of North East England's most important modern icons - **The Angel of the North**. Commissioned by Gateshead Council and created by renowned sculptor Antony Gormley, this huge statue, made from 200 tonnes of steel, is 65 feet high and has a wingspan of 175 feet. It was erected in February 1998, and has attracted world-wide attention.

The **Gateshead Quay Visitor Centre** is housed in the former St Mary's parish

The Angel of The North

BEAMISH MUSEUM

Beamish, County Durham DH9 0RG
Tel:01207 231811 Fax: 01207 290933
website: merlins.demon.co.uk/beamish
e-mail: museum@beamish.org.uk

No trip to County Durham is complete without a trip to the award-winning **North of England Open Air Museum at Beamish**. Set in 200 acres of countryside, it illustrates life in the North of England in the late 19th and early 20th centuries. There is so much to see. Stroll down a cobbled street

full of shops, banks and offices, visit an old Methodist chapel, find out how life was lived on a farm in the late 19th century, take a trip on a tram or steam train, visit an old dentist's surgery (and be grateful you didn't live in those days, and needed a filling!), walk through a colliery village, and go down a drift mine, As this is County Durham, cradle of the railways, you can also see the world's third oldest surviving railway engine, which dates from 1822, housed in a specially created created Great Engine Shed. There's also Pockerley Manor and Horse Yard, based on a small fortified manor house. Here you experience life as it was lived 200 years ago. Stroll the terraced gardens, walk through the fine horse yard, and see the costumes from all these years ago.

Beamish is justly famous as a great day out for all the family. Reasonably priced meals and snacks are available, and there's a friendly shop where you can buy souvenirs.

Opening Times: April-October 10.00-17.00 (last admission 15.00); November-March 10.00-16.00; closed Mondays and Fridays; Admission charge

church, where there is a display on Gateshead's history and future. It also incorporates a tourist information centre.

Due to open in 2003 is the **Gateshead Music Centre**, a £62 million project which will provide world-class facilities on a site overlooking the Tyne. There are plans for a 1650-seat auditorium, a 450-seat secondary hall and a school of music. It will cater for all tastes - jazz, classical, folk and rock. Close by will be the **Baltic Centre for Contemporary Arts**, due to open in 2002. Based in an old grain warehouse on the banks of the Tyne, it will be the largest centre of its kind in Britain outside London. Linking the two will be a £30 million leisure complex with an 18 screen cinema, bowling alley, nightclubs, fitness suits and restaurants.

But perhaps the most spectacular new attraction in Gateshead is the £21 million **Gateshead Millennium Bridge**, erected across the Tyne, and due for opening in 2001. Designed to take cyclists and pedestrians, it will allow ships to pass underneath. Its operation has been likened to a giant blinking eye.

AROUND GATESHEAD

BEAMISH
6 miles SW of Gateshead on the A693

The award-winning **North of England Open Air Museum** is situated in 300 acres of landscaped parkland at Beamish, and here early life in County Durham has been vividly re-created. This is one of the county's major tourist attractions, with many features which were rescued from locations around County Durham - and even further afield - and re-erected on site (see panel on page 32).

Two miles to the NW is **Causey Arch**, claimed to be the world's first single-arch railway bridge. It was designed by Ralph Wood, a local stonemason, and carried the **Tanfield Railway** - opened in 1725 - between Sunniside and Causey. In those days the wagons were pulled by horses, though steam power eventually took over. Trains now run along three miles of line between Sunniside and East Tanfield. There is a car park and picnic area close by, and rights of way link them to Beamish.

CONSETT
12 miles SW of Gateshead on the A692

Steel-making first started in this area of County Durham at **Shotley Bridge**, when craftsmen from Germany set up their furnaces in the 17th century and began making swords and cutlery. When the railway came here to serve the local iron works and surrounding collieries in the 19th century, Shotley Bridge began to develop something of a reputation as a spa town, and its popularity as such is evident from the many fine houses to be seen here, such as Dial House.

Steel-making on the grand scale began in Consett in 1840, when the Derwent Iron Company built two blast furnaces. By 1890 over 7,500 people were employed in the industry, and over 1 million tonnes of steel were being produced. In the late 1960s, 6,000 people were still employed in the steelworks, though this wasn't to last. The demand for steel dropped, and in 1980 the works closed forever.

Consett is now cleaning itself up. Land reclamation schemes have cleaned up the area where the steelworks once stood, and its attendant spoil heaps are green hillocks dotted with young trees. However, the countryside outside the town has some interesting places which can be visited.

A redundant railway line north of the town is linked to **The Derwent Walk Country Park**. The park covers 425 acres of woodland and riverside meadow, and the Derwent Walk itself is the track bed of the old Derwent Valley Railway between Consett and Swalwell. The main walk is 11 miles long, and suitable for cycles, horses and wheelchairs. It gives access to a number of paths which include nature trails, the South Tyne Cycleway and the Heritage Way. Swalwell Visitor Centre, situated at the northern end of the Derwent Walk, is the starting point for a history trail and this centre also has a large pond and

PATH HEAD WATER MILL

Summerhill, Blaydon on Tyne NE21 4SP
Tel: 0191 414 6288 website:
www.gatesheadmill.co.uk
e-mail: (enquiries) enquiries@gatesheadmill.co.uk
(bookings) bookings@gatesheadmill.co.uk
For many years, the 18th century **Path Head Water Mill** lay abandoned and neglected. Then, in 1995, it was decided to restore it to its full working glory. In 1998 it opened to the public, though there is still a lot of work to be done. It is located in a picturesque, quiet
dell, and here you can see how water was the main source of energy before the advent of the steam engine, and how a mill harnessed the power of water to turn its machinery. A small gallery of photographs shows you the stages in the mill's restoration, plus there's a tearoom. Opening Times: Tuesday-Sunday 10.00-15.00 in winter and 9.30-17.30 in summer; Closed Mondays, except for bank holidays; Admission charge

THE JOLLY DROVERS

Redwell Hills, Leadgate, Consett, Durham DH8 6RR
Tel: 01207 503994

As the name suggests, lead and gate have been combined to give the village of Leadgate, just outside Consett, its name. Lead was transported between Weardale and the Tyne and it is believed that there was a tollgate here at one time. In the heart of the village stands **The Jolly Drovers**, an attractive inn with a superb central location. Dating back to 1780 this was originally an ale house which has been much extended over the years resulting in the building you see today.

The interior is well planned, spacious and comfortable with three lounge and restaurant areas, each with an open fire to keep customer nice and warm in the cooler months. Food is served throughout

from a menu offering a good selection of snacks and main dishes each lunch time and evening. The dishes are well priced and prepared using fresh, locally sourced ingredients. Behind the bar they stock a range of beer, lager and real ales, with the best seller being John Smiths.

The outdoor beer garden is a popular spot for enjoying a refreshing drink in summer months and there are some stunning views over the surrounding countryside. There is regular entertainment provided with live musicians and a regular quiz night.

butterfly garden. There is another visitors centre at Thornley Woodlands.

The local council has produced a small guidebook outlining various walks - none more than six and a half miles long - near the town. To the south west of Consett, almost in the North Pennines, is **Allensford Park**. It sits off the A68, on the County Durham and Northumberland border, and on the banks of the

Gibside Estate

Derwent. It has a picnic park, caravan site and woodland walks. **Deneburn Wood**, a ten acre plot of woodland with some delightful walks, has wood carvings by well known sculptor David Gross.

To the south of the town is **Hownsgill Viaduct**, constructed in 1857 to take the track of the Stanhope and Tyne Railway. Visitors can now walk across it, and there are some spectacular views.

EBCHESTER
10 miles SW of Gateshead on the A694

Ebchester is the site of a Roman fort called Vindomora, and some scant remains can be seen in the churchyard of **St Ebba's Church**. It was one of a string of forts on Dere Street, the Roman road which linked York with the north. Inside the church are a number of inscribed Roman stones, including an altar to the god Jupiter, "the greatest and the best".

GIBSIDE CHAPEL
6 miles SW of Gateshead on the A694

The large mansion at **Gibside Estate** was owned by the Bowes family, and

partially demolished in 1958. Now the place is chiefly visited for the Palladian Gibside Chapel, owned by the National Trust. Work began on building it in 18th century, although it wasn't finally consecrated until 1812.

It's a stately building, looking more like a small mansion than a church, and was built for Sir George Bowes, whose mausoleum lies beneath it. It is open from April to October, and once a month a church service is held.

JARROW
4 miles E of Gateshead on the A184/A194

Mixed memories surround the town of Jarrow. Once a thriving centre for the Tyneside shipbuilding industry, it gained fame during the famous **Jarrow Hunger March** when hundreds of unemployed men from the area walked to London to draw attention to their plight. A bas-relief at the Metro Station commemorates the event, which took place in 1936.

Jarrow, however, has a happier side. During the 7th century, Northumbria was a kingdom in its own right, and a shining beacon of learning and

Christianity in these islands. Nowhere is this shown more clearly shown than in **Bede's World**, a museum and outdoor interpretation centre. It encompasses both a monastery and church which were founded in the 7th century and dedicated to St Paul by Benedict Biscop, plus a new museum building and a re-creation of an Anglo Saxon farm. The original dedication stone of **St Paul's Church** can still be seen within its

Souter Lighthouse

original chancel, showing the date of 23 April AD685, together with fragments of Anglo-Saxon stained glass which scientific tests have established to be the oldest ecclesiastical stained glass in Europe, if not the world. It was here, at Jarrow monastery in the 7th and 8th centuries, that Bede wrote his famous "Ecclesiastical History of England". He was undoubtedly Britain's first genuine historian, employing methods of checking and double checking his information that are still in use today. An ancient chair in the chancel of St Paul's is said to be his, but this is doubtful. **Jarrow Hall** is a Georgian building which has been incorporated into the museum.

MARSDEN
9 miles E of Gateshead on the A183

The coast between South Shields and Roker is magnificent, with rocky cliffs projecting into the sea at Lizard Point and the impressive Marsden Bay. **Marsden Rock** was once a famous County Durham landmark - a rock

formation shaped like an arc de triomphe which stood in the bay. In 1996, however, it finally succumbed to nature and collapsed, leaving two tall stumps. The smaller stump proved so unstable that in 1997 it was demolished.

Souter Lighthouse at Lizard Point was built in 1871, and was the first reliable electric lighthouse in the world. It's a perfect example of Victorian technology, and features an engine room, fog horns and lighthouse keeper's living quarters. It is open to the public, and owned by the National Trust.

SOUTH SHIELDS
8 miles E of Gateshead on the A184/A194

South Shields stretches out along the southern shore of the Tyne estuary. Though close to Newcastle and Gateshead, the North Sea coastline here is remarkably unspoiled, and can be walked along for many miles. No less a personage than King George V declared that the beach at South Shields was the finest he had seen. This is a stretch of fine firm sand behind which a small but pleasant resort thrives.

However, it is the older part of South Shields that has given the town a new claim to fame, thanks to the work of one of the world's most popular novelists - Dame Catherine Cookson, who died in 1998. She was born Katie McMullen in 1906, in a house in Leam Lane amid poverty and squalor, the illegitimate child of a woman called Kate Fawcett. The house is gone now, but a plaque has been erected marking the spot.

Catherine Cookson wrote a series of popular novels - the world sales are in now in excess of 120 million - which captured the world of her own childhood, and that of her parents and grandparents, with vivid clarity. It was a world which was shaped in the 19th century around the narrow streets and coal-mines - a world of class warfare and conflict, passion and tragedy, violence and reconciliation.

A **Catherine Cookson Trail** has been now laid out in the town, showing places associated with her and her books, and a leaflet is available to guide you round. There is also a Catherine Cookson exhibition in the **South Shields Museum**.

The mean streets she describes no longer exist. The old Town Hall is now part of a pedestrianised area, served by a station on the Tyneside Metro, and the town has a clean, modern image.

In Baring Street you can see the extensive remains of the 2nd-century Roman fort, **Arbeia**. The West Gate has been faithfully reconstructed to match what experts believe to be its original appearance, with two three-storey towers, two gates and side walls. It is the biggest reconstruction of its kind in the country, and a truly magnificent achievement. It also incorporates the **Commander's Accommodation and Barracks**.

Much of the old harbour area at South Shields is now being restored, particularly around the **Mill Dam** area along the riverside, where fine Georgian buildings and warehouses survive. The river itself, like all great river estuaries, is a constant fascination as boats come around the breakwaters into the spectacular mouth of the Tyne heading for one of the docks, a reminder of the importance of the Tyneside ports.

SPRINGWELL
3 miles S of Gateshead on the B1288

Springwell is home to the **Bowes Railway**, once a private rail system pulling coal-filled wagons from pit to port. The original wagonways would originally have been of wood, with horses pulling the wagons. The line finally closed in 1974, and now part has been reopened as an industrial heritage centre, jointly owned by Gateshead and Sunderland Councils.

Many of the buildings of the original Springwell Colliery have been retained, as well as the hauliers houses at Blackham Hill. There are guided tours and trips on some of the trains.

SUNDERLAND

Sunderland is one of Britain's newer cities, and much of its history is told in an exhibition in the **Winter Gardens and Sunderland Museum and Art Gallery** in Burdon Road, where examples of works by Lowry and J.W. Carmichael, plus the maritime paintings of Sunderland-born Royal Academician and theatre-set designer Clarkson Stanfield are on display. The place has recently been completely refurbished, and is due to open in the summer of 2001. The Winter Gardens is a green

RYHOPE ENGINES MUSEUM

Ryhope Pumping Station, Ryhope, Sunderland SR2 0ND
Tel: 0191 521 0235 website: www.g3wte.demon.co.uk

The **Ryhope Engines Museum** is within the old Ryhope Pumping Station, three miles south of Sunderland city centre. The station was built in 1868, and is a superb example of how Victorian engineers managed to combine what was then cutting edge technology with functional yet elegantly simple architecture. It was here that water was pumped from deep within the ground to supply both Sunderland and the surrounding areas with a good, fresh supply. The station was built by the old Sunderland and South Shields Water Company, which was formed as a direct result of the many cholera outbreaks in the early 19th century. But it wasn't just the public that demanded a reliable source of water. Industry was flourishing in the area at the time, and they too were supplied from the station.

In 1967 the station closed, and three years later a group of local people decided to try and preserve an important piece of the area's history by taking it over and keeping the machinery in good working order. The station consists of two 100hp beam steam engines in parallel, connected to four pumps. Two of the pumps lifted three million gallons of water a day from 250 feet deep wells by means of long rods sunk into the well shafts. The water was then transferred to two further wells called staple wells, which were only 140 feet deep, and the other two pumps lifted this water to the surface.

Though the process might appear simple, the design of the buildings and machinery was not without problems. The engines and pumps are massively heavy, so the station's foundations had to be deep and strong to support them as well as the brick-built walls. The moving beams, which were over 33 feet long, were pivoted 22 feet above the floor, and all this had to be accounted for when the walls and floors were being built, as they all form an integrated structure.

On certain days of the year, the Ryhope boilers are stoked up, and the pump beams start working. They rock at an even 10 strokes per minute, and it is fascinating to see them in motion. Even after all these years they still work perfectly, even though they don't raise water any more.

Also within the station is a fascinating museum (within the old coal house!) about water pumping, supply and use, and a display called "Clean and Decent" which shows some fascinating articles of sanitary ware through the ages. There's a small shop where books and plans can be bought, and there's ample parking.

Opening Times: Easter until the end of December; static: Sunday 14.00-16.30; working: Easter: Friday to Monday: 11.00-16.30 Spring and Autumn holidays: 11.00-16.30. There are two further working weekends during the year. Telephone for dates; Admission charge

oasis in a glass rotunda, with exotic plants from all over the world. All are contained within **Mowbray Park**, which has been fully restored with themed walkways, poetry inscriptions, historical monuments, a lake and a bowling green. In the summer months, there is a full programme of entertainments. On Ryhope Road, south of the city centre, is the university-owned **Vardy Art Gallery** (see panel below).

The **Exchange Building**, the oldest public building in the city, has recently been refurbished, and is now a venue for the whole community to enjoy. Exhibitions, meetings and functions take place there, plus there is a restaurant and café. And the famous **Empire Theatre** - a Sunderland institution - can still be enjoyed. Recent improvements have made it one of the top theatres in the North east.

St Michael and All Angels Church on High Street West is worth visiting for one reason - it's the first minster to be created in England since the Reformation. It was proclaimed **Sunderland Minster** in January 1998 to celebrate the town's elevation to city status.

Three miles south of the city centre is the **Ryhope Engines Museum**, based on a pumping station which supplied the city and surrounding areas with water (see panel opposite).

On the north side of the Wear, in the suburb of Monkwearmouth, is **St Peter's Church**, one of the most important sites of early Christianity in the country. This tiny Saxon church was founded in AD674 by Benedict Biscop, a Northumbrian nobleman and thane of King Oswy, who had travelled to Rome and was inspired to found a monastery on his return. This was to become a great centre of culture and learning, rivalled only by Jarrow. The Venerable Bede, England's first great historian, lived and worked here for a time and described the monastery's foundation in his "Ecclesiastical History of England". The west tower and the wall of this most fascinating church have survived from Saxon times and the area around the church, where shipyards once stood, has been landscaped.

Close by, in Liberty Way, is the **National Glass Centre**. Glass was first made in Sunderland in the 7th century at St Peter's Church, so it's fitting that the centre was built here. Visitors can see how glass was made all those years ago, and watch modern glassblowing. There is a Glass Gallery, devoted to all forms of glass art, and in the Kaleidoscope Gallery there are plenty of interactive exhibits showing glass's many amazing properties. Walking on the roof is not for the faint hearted, as it's made of clear glass panels 30 feet above the riverside. However, some

VARDY ART GALLERY

University of Sunderland, Backhouse Park, Ryhope Road, Sunderland SR2 7EF
Tel: 0191 515 2128

Founded in 1988, the **Vardy Art Gallery** forms part of the University of Sunderland's School of Arts, Design and Media. It hosts a varied programme of exhibitions by talented artists and craft workers, as well as regular talks, gallery tours, workshops and art classes for children and adults. During term time, light meals and refreshments are available. The gallery is a ten minutes walk from the city centre. Opening times: 10.00-17.00 Monday to Friday; Free

National Glass Centre

Monkwearmouth Station is one of the most handsome small railway stations in the British Isles. Built in imposing neo-classical style, it looks more like a temple or a town hall. Trains no longer call here, and it has been converted into a small museum of the Victorian railway age.

Roker is one of Sunderland's suburbs, located to the north of the great breakwaters that form the city's harbour. The northern breakwater, known as **Roker Pier**, is 825 metres long and was opened in 1903. Roker Park has been carefully restored to its former Victorian splendour, and from Roker and Seaburn through to Sunderland there is a six-mile-long seaside promenade.

panels are opaque, so people with vertigo can still walk there and enjoy the view.

It is worth making your way to Roker to visit **St Andrew's Church** in Talbot Road, described as "the Cathedral of the Arts and Crafts Movement". Built early this century, it is crammed with

THE RED LION

North Road, Plawsworth,
Nr. Chester-le-Street,
County Durham DH2 3NL
Tel: 0191 371 0253
e-mail patriciaredlion@eol.com

The small village of Plawsworth can be easily located just off the A697 a couple of miles south of Chester-le-Street. Since it was built in the 1902, The Red Lion has been something of a landmark for travellers in the area. Built in a classic Georgian style the property is sure to stand the test of time, and

a conservatory dining room, in a matching style, has recently been added.

Comfortable, reasonably priced accommodation can sometimes be difficult to find but if you are in need of somewhere to stay then look no further. Here there are five en-suite guest bedrooms of varying sizes and the master bedroom even features a Jacuzzi. All the rooms are comfortably and individually furnished and provided with a colour TV and tea and coffee making facilities.

Downstairs you will find a large lounge bar with a good sized separate restaurant attached seating up to 150. The menu offers a superb choice of freshly prepared and home cooked dishes all served in decent portions and reasonably priced. The Sunday lunch is especially good value for money at only £3.95 per head. To complement your meal there is an extensive wine selection together with a choice of real ales being stocked behind the bar.

treasures by the leading craftsmen of the period - silver lectern, pulpit and altar furniture by Ernest Gimson, the font by Randall Wells, stained-glass in the east window by H.A. Payne, a painted chancel ceiling by Macdonald Gill, stone tablets engraved by Eric Gill, and Burne-Jones tapestry and carpets from the William Morris workshops.

Art of another kind is to be found in the **Sculpture Trail**. It was established in 1990, and has placed various works of outdoor sculpture along the banks of the Wear - mostly on the Monkwearmouth side. A leaflet has been produced that explains the exhibits as visitors go round.

By the beginning of 2002, Sunderland will be linked to the Tyneside Metro system, with stations at Sunderland Central, Monkwearmouth, the University, the Stadium of Light (Sunderland AFC's new ground) and Park Lane Transport Interchange.

AROUND SUNDERLAND

CHESTER-LE-STREET
8 miles SW of Sunderland on the A167

Chester-le-Street is a busy market town built around the confluence of Cong Burn and the River Wear. The street on which the town once stood was a Roman road, later replaced by the Great North Road. As the name suggests, there was a Roman fort here at one time.

The medieval **St Mary's and St Cuthbert's Church**, is built on the site of a cathedral established in AD883 by the monks of Lindisfarne carrying the body of St Cuthbert. His coffin rested here for 113 years until the monks took it to its final resting place at Durham. There are no less than 14 effigies (not all

of them genuine) of members of the Lumley family within the church, though they don't mark the sites of their graves. Next to the church is the **Ankers House Museum**, situated in the medieval anchorite. Between 1383 and 1547, various anchorites, or Christian hermits, lived here at one time or another.

Lumley Castle, to the east across the River Wear, was built in 1389 by Sir Ralph Lumley, whose descendant, Sir Richard Lumley, became the 1st Earl of Scarborough in the 1690's. In the early 18th century it was refashioned by the architect Vanbrugh for the 2nd Earl, and turned into a magnificent stately home. But gradually the castle fell out of favour with the Lumley family, and they chose to stay in their estates in Yorkshire instead. For a while it was owned by Durham University until turned into the luxurious hotel it is today.

Waldridge Fell Country Park, two miles south west of Chester-le-Street and close to Waldridge village, is County Durham's last surviving area of lowland heathland. A car park and signed footpaths give access to over 300 acres of open countryside, rich in natural history.

PENSHAW
4 miles W of Sunderland off the A183

This mining village is famous for the **Penshaw Monument**, a fanciful Grecian temple modelled on the Temple of Theseus, and built in 1844 in memory of the John George Lambton, 1st Earl of Durham and Governor of Canada. A waymarked circular walk of just over three miles links Penshaw Monument with natural and industrial features of the River Wear.

All Saints Church dates from 1745,

and has one unusual feature - inside it there is a monument to the Eliot family carved on a piece of stone from the Pyramid of Cheops in Egypt.

To the west is **Lambton Castle**, scene of an old legend about a huge worm - **The Lambton Worm** - that terrorised the area. It seems that, many years go, the heir to the Lambton estate was fishing in the Wear one Sunday morning when he should have been at worship. Instead of a fish, he caught a huge worm, which he promptly threw into a well, where it grew to an enormous size. So big did it become, in fact, that it eventually terrorised the neighbourhood and could even coil itself round hillsides. The heir, however, knew nothing of this, as he was away the Holy Land fighting in the Crusades. On his return, however, he met a witch who gave him the secret of how the worm could be killed. He must wade deep into the river wearing protective armour then kill the first living thing he met. If he didn't, no Lambton would die peacefully in his or her bed for nine generations. His father, hearing of this, released an old dog close by. Unfortunately, the young heir saw his father first, and refused to kill him. He did go on to kill the huge creature eventually, but the witch's prophesy about the next nine generations came true.

SEAHAM
4 miles S of Sunderland on the B1287

Seaham was developed by the Marquises of Londonderry. In 1821 the family bought what was then the old village of Seaham, for the purpose of building a harbour from which to transport coal from the family's collieries to London and the Continent. The present town grew up around the harbour, and although most of the collieries have now closed, Seaham is still very much a working town.

All that now remains of the original village is **St Mary the Virgin Church** (some parts of which dates from Saxon times), its vicarage, and **Seaham Hall** on the northern outskirts of the town. This was once the home of the Milbanke family, where in 1815 Lord Byron met and married Anne Isabella Milbanke - a marriage that was to last for only one year.

WASHINGTON
6 miles W of Sunderland on the A1231

Present-day Washington is a new town with modern, self-sufficient districts scattered over a wide area surrounding the town centre. The town was built to attract industry into an area whose mining industry was in decline, and in this it has succeeded. The architecture is uninspiring, though within the old village of Washington to the east of the town centre there is one attraction well worth visiting - **Washington Old Hall**, ancestral home of the Washington family, ancestors of George Washington, the first American president.

People tend to think that Sulgrave Manor in Northamptonshire was the Washingtons' ancestral home, but the family only lived there for about 100 years. Before that they had been in Lancashire and Westmorland, and before that they had lived at Washington Hall for 430 years.

The Hall was originally a manor house built in the 12th century for the de Wessington family, whose descendants through a female line finally quit the house in 1613, when it was acquired by the Bishop of Durham.

The present house, in local sandstone, was rebuilt on the medieval foundations

Washington Old Hall

preservation committee managed to save it, thanks to money from across the Atlantic. In 1955 it was officially reopened by the American Ambassador and two years later it was acquired by the National Trust. The interiors recreate a typical manor house of the 17th century, and there are some items on display which are connected to George Washinton himself, though the man never visited or stayed there.

Washington is also the home to the **Washington Wildfowl and Wetlands Centre**, a conservation area and bird watchers' paradise covering some 100 acres of ponds, lakes and woodland sloping down to the River Wear. There are over 1,200 birds representing 105 different species, including mallard, widgeon, nene (the state bird of Hawaii), heron, Chilean flamingos, redshank and lapwing. There is also the **Glaxo Wellcome Wetland Discovery Centre**, with displays and exhibits, hides, a waterfowl nursery, an adventure play area and the Waterside Café.

in about 1623. In 1936 it was to be demolished, but a hastily formed

3 Weardale, Teesdale and the Pennines

To the west, County Durham sweeps up to the Northern Pennines, a hauntingly beautiful area of moorland, high fells and deep, green dales. Part of the Pennine Way cuts through County Durham in the south, close to Barnard Castle and even closer to Middleton-in-Teesdale. It then follows Upper Teesdale west until it enters Cumbria. Further north, it enters Northumberland to the west of Haltwhistle and then enters the Northumberland National Park.

High Force, River Tees

As it passes through Teesdale, it goes past the waterfalls of Low Force, High Force, and, south of Cow Green Reservoir, Cauldron Snout. These are magical places, and show just how water has shaped the Durham Dales.

From about Blanchland and Cowshill northwards, part of this area is in Northumberland. But it all makes up one homogeneous whole - a part of the country that has been called "England's last wilderness". It's also been officially designated as an "Area of Outstanding Natural Beauty". This is where tumbling mountain streams have cut deep into the rock, creating impressive waterfalls. The great northern rivers of the Wear, the Tees, the Tyne and the Derwent have their sources here, and the area is rich in wildlife. Hen harriers breed here, as do merlins and other rare species, and in spring and summer the plaintive call of the curlew can be heard.

The whole area seems to have been made for walking, though in the winter months it can be wild and inhospitable. There are plenty of rights-of-way to be explored, and new cycle routes have been laid out, including the **C2C** (coast to coast) cycle path, with leaflets available for those who

Rock Climbing, Tarset Burn

wish to make use of them.

But man has left his mark here as well. The lower reaches have been farmed for centuries, and the high fells are home to many flocks of sheep. At one time there were even woollen mills at Barnard Castle, which provided a ready market for local sheep farmers. Lead mining was a thriving industry, with mines being located at such places as Killhope, Ireshopeburn and St John's Chapel. Middleton-in-Teesdale was even the headquarters of the London Lead Company, a great Quaker business venture.

There are two great County Durham dales - Teesdale to the south and Weardale to the north. Of the two, Teesdale is the softer, at least in its lower reaches, having an affinity with the Yorkshire Dales to the south. This isn't surprising, for at one time part of the River Tees formed the boundary between County Durham and Yorkshire. It's dotted with lovely villages and small towns such as Barnard Castle and Middleton-in Teesdale. Beyond Middleton-in-Teesdale, however, the B6277 winds up and over some bleak but beautiful scenery until it arrives at Alston in Cumbria, England's highest market town.

The A689, which winds its way through Weardale further north, also takes you to Alston, but it takes you through a dale that at first sight seems less interesting than its neighbour. The houses and villages seem grittier, somehow. The landscape suggests that the bones of England have been exposed to view. Life, at one time, must have been harsh here.

Fishing near Barnard Castle

But there is still plenty to see, such as the lead mining museum at Killhope, the curious fossilised tree stump at Stanhope, and the village of Blanchland, a few miles to the north in Derwentdale.

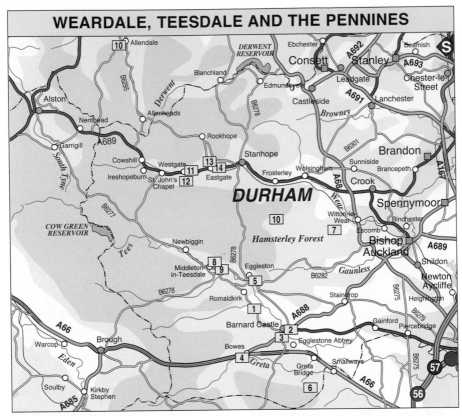

WEARDALE, TEESDALE AND THE PENNINES

© MAPS IN MINUTES ™ (1999)

PLACES TO STAY, EAT, DRINK AND SHOP

BARNARD CASTLE

This old market town is a natural centre for exploring the central part of Teesdale. It is recognised as one of the 51 most important towns in Great Britain as far as history and architecture are concerned. It owes its existence to **Barnard Castle** itself, founded in the 12th century by Bernard, son of Guy de Baliol, one of the knights who fought alongside William I. This family's most famous - or infamous - son was King John Baliol, Edward I's puppet king of Scotland.

The ruins, with the massive, round keep overlooking the town's narrow, arched bridge of 1569 over the Tees, have a gaunt beauty. The castle has experienced its share of incidents, perhaps most spectacularly during the ill-fated Catholic Rising of the North in 1569. At that time it was besieged by rebel forces for 11 days and, although it was finally forced to capitulate, this gave sufficient time for Queen Elizabeth's army, under the Earl of Sussex, to speed to York and force the rebels to flee. Many were executed and those leading families who had supported the plans to overthrow Elizabeth I lost their lands.

The town has an especially rich architectural heritage, with handsome houses, cottages, shops and inns dating from the 17th to the 19th centuries. There is an impressive **Market Cross** and an old town hall contained within an unusual octagonal structure, built in 1747. The area under the veranda has been variously used as a butter market, fire station or gaol, and the first floor as a courthouse. You can still see the bullet holes in the weather-vane, resulting from a wager by two local men in 1804, shooting from outside the Turk's Head,

DOE PARK

Cotherstone, Barnard Castle, County Durham DL12 9UQ
Tel: 01833 650302 Fax: 01833 650302

Doe Park is a family-run touring caravan site located near to Cotherstone in Teesdale. The site is located within the grounds of an impressive 17th century house which is home to Muriel and Keith Lamb. The pleasant situation within the peaceful, sheltered parkland enjoys some fine views over the surrounding dales and moorland and the fields are also easily accessed from the road. The 72 level pitches, some with hard standing, are generously spaced. There are electric hook-ups for all and the whole site is well lit at night. Visitors will also find modern, heated toilet and

shower blocks, with full disabled facilities, a washing up room and laundry room with washer and tumble dryer. A small site shop sells calor gas, battery charging service, fresh milk and eggs while the village of Cotherstone is only half a mile away and has a post office and shop with a more extensive range.

There is plenty to see and do for visitors to this part of the North Pennines. A nature reserve, which forms part of Doe Park farm, adjoins the caravan park, Upper Teesdale is an Area of Outstanding Natural Beauty and is well worth exploring while the city of Durham is only a 45 minute drive. Open March to October.

100 yards away, to determine who was the best shot. The building was fully restored in 1999.

A walk along Newgate will bring you to the **Bowes Museum**, surely one of the most spectacular buildings in England. It looks like a French chateau, and is completely unexpected in a small English market town. It holds collections of paintings and objets d'art that are of international importance (see panel below).

If visitors strike out along the A66 west of Barnard Castle, they'll

BOWES MUSEUM

Barnard Castle, County Durham DL12 8NP
Tel: 01833 690606 Fax: 01833 637163
website: www.bowesmuseum.org.uk e-mail: info@bowesmuseum.org.uk

The Bowes Museum is one of County Durham's great surprises - a beautiful and grand French chateau-style museum on the outskirts of the historic town of Barnard Castle. It was built by John Bowes, illegitimate son of the 10th Earl of Strathmore, and his Parisian actress wife, Josephine Beni™te, Countess of Montalbo, between 1862 and 1875. They wanted to house the vast collection of works of

art they had amassed from all corners of Europe so that people from all walks of life could see and enjoy them, but unfortunately they died before their dream was realised.

But realised it eventually was, and today it has an outstanding collection that will take your breath away. County Durham is lucky to have a such a museum and gallery - one that is undoubtedly of international importance. Here the visitor can admire a vast range objets d'arts and paintings, including what is acknowledged to be the most important collection of Spanish paintings in Britain. There are works by by Goya and El Greco, and works by painters of the calibre of Canaletto, Boudin and Tiepola can also be found on the walls. Tapestries, ceramics, woodwork, fine furniture and clocks can also be seen - a feast of the finest craftsmanship that could be found in Europe at the time. But John and Josephine Bowes didn't just restrict themselves to the grand and the prestigious. There is also a wonderful display of toys, including the world's first toy train set.

The Museum's most famous exhibit is undoubtedly the Silver Swan. The life-sized bird, with its exquisite silver plumage, is an automaton and musical box, set in a stream made from twisted glass rods with small fish "swimming" among them. When it is would up, the glass rods rotate, a tinkling tune is played, and the swan preens itself before lowering its head towards the water and seemingly picking up a fish. It then raises its head once more and appears to swallows it.

The museum is under the care of Durham County Council, and runs a regular programme of temporary exhibitions and displays. There are also occasional craft fairs and musical events (programme available from the Museum), plus special free guided tours.The licensed café sells snacks and light meals, and there's a shop where you can buy a souvenir or gift. Parking is free, and, apart from one or two areas, the museum is disabled-friendly.

Opening Times: 11.00-17.00 daily, except Christmas Day, Boxing Day and New Year's Day; Admission charge

eventually reach the small Cumbrian town of Brough. It was near this road that King Edmund erected the **Reys Cross** to mark the boundary between the kingdom of Northumbria and what was then the Scottish province of Cumbria.

The Dales, nr Barnard Castle

AROUND BARNARD CASTLE

BOWES
4 miles W of Barnard Castle off the A66

This small village is the site of a Roman fort called Lavatrae. The castle was built for Henry 11 in the 12th century, and the church has Roman stones built into its fabric. Charles Dickens visited the village while researching material for "Nicholas Nickleby", and noticed a boys' academy run by William Shaw in the main street. This became the model for

THE MONTALBO HOTEL

Montalbo Street, Barnard Castle,
County Durham
Tel: 01833 637342
e-mail montalbo@teesdaleonline

The Montalbo Hotel can be located in the heart of the old market town of Barnard Castle on the road of the same name. This well established hostelry dates back to the mid-17th century and has been serving the local community for over 350 years, though not always with alcoholic beverages as it was a temperance hotel for a number of years! The building is quite plain in style and constructed of local stone to last for centuries. The interior is warm and bright and kept spotlessly clean with the walls being decorated with a collection of military shields. Food is served each evening with a traditional roast lunch served on Sundays. The dishes use fresh local produce and are home cooked and prepared to order. The bar stocks a good range of beer and lager with Theakstons and a guest cask ale always on tap. Entertainment is provided in the form of a regular quiz nights.

Accommodation is available with a total of seven guest rooms, all en-suite and provided with a TV and hot drinks tray. The rates are very reasonable and this would make an ideal base for a touring holiday or short break. Speciality tennis and golfing breaks can also be arranged. Booking well in advance is to be strongly recommended.

THE ANCIENT UNICORN INN

Bowes, Barnard Castle,
County Durham DL12 9HL
Tel: 01833 628321 Fax: 01833 628321
e-mail management@ancient_unicorn.co.uk
website www.ancient_unicorn.co.uk

The attractive village of Bowes is where visitors will find the most charming **Ancient Unicorn Inn**. This attractive, stone built inn is Grade 2 listed and dates back as far as the 15th century. The main structure of the building, and much of the interior as well, is mostly unchanged retaining many original features and much of the character. Attracting a loyal following from the community of Bowes, it is not surprising that many visitors to the area also find themselves attracted to the Ancient Unicorn. The spacious interior can accommodate the many customers with ease, and everyone will be able to find a table at which to enjoy a refreshing drink or a tasty meal.

The bar stocks the usual range of drinks with up to three guest cask ales which are regularly rotated. The food which is on offer is home prepared from local produce resulting in a superb varied menu of meals and snacks to suit all tastes. All visitors are sure to find something to suit their tastes and vegetarians are well catered for. Live entertainment is provided with regular quiz nights and drama sessions, with short plays regularly being performed for the enjoyment of all. Accommodation is provided with one family room, four self-contained en-suite units and a ramblers' bunk room sleeping six. Ring for full details.

THE THREE TUNS INN

Church Bank, Eggleston,
Durham DL12 0AH
Tel: 01833 650289

Eggleston is a lovely village on the north bank of the Tees, seven miles to the north west of Barnard Castle. Many of the houses date back to the 18th century though the village itself is still growing as it is a desirable place in which to live. Eggleston Hall just north of the medieval bridge heading towards Romaldkirk has some beautiful gardens which are open to the public.

The Three Tuns Inn is one of the many fine 18th century buildings in the village and is an excellent example of period architecture which has been well preserved and maintained. The building is steeped in character while having also been updated to provide a comfortable environment in which today's customers can enjoy a quiet drink and a bite to eat. The decor features the original stone floors and exposed beams while open fires keep the interior cosy and warm. Many regular visitors are drawn here by the high quality and variety of food on offer each lunchtime and evening. The menu certainly has a very broad choice catering to all appetites and tastes. Meals can be taken in the separate restaurant which is called The Teesdale because of the magnificent views that it offers over the valley. The bar also stocks a good range of cask ales, beer and lager to enjoy with your meal.

Recently under new management, The Three Tuns is for the first time able to offer bed and breakfast accommodation with four en-suite rooms available from Spring 2001. The owners also run a fudge shop in Berwick so don't forget to ask to try some of their home-made produce!

"Dotheboys Hall", and Shaw became Wackford Squeers. In the churchyard is buried George Taylor, his inspiration for Smike. "I think," Dickens later said, "his ghost put Smike into my head upon the spot."

EGGLESTON
6 miles NW of Barnard Castle on the B6281

Within the grounds of Eggleston Hall are the

Egglestone Abbey

Eggleston Hall Gardens, which are open to the public all year (apart from Christmas Day and Boxing Day). There are four acres of garden here within the high wall which once enclosed the kitchen garden. They are laid out informally, with many rare herbaceous plants and shrubs to be seen. Close by are the ruins of an old church which can be explored.

EGGLESTONE ABBEY
2 miles S of Barnard Castle, near the A66

Egglestone Abbey is not far from the village of Boldron, and easily reached by a riverside footpath. It is made up of the ruins of a Premonstratensian abbey of which most of the nave and chancel, built in the 13th and 14th century, survives. This was only a small monastic settlement but it enjoys a superb setting above the River Tees.

GRETA BRIDGE
4 miles SE of Barnard Castle on the A66

Lovers of romantic landscape should make their way south of Barnard Castle to Greta Bridge on the A66, the graceful old bridge immortalised in paintings by great English water-colourists such as Cotman and Turner. Footpaths lead by the riverside, through the edge of **Rokeby Park.** Close by are the ruins of medieval **Mortham Tower,** subject of Sir Walter Scott's narrative poem of colourful chivalry and courtly love,

Rokeby Hall

WILSON HOUSE

Barningham, Richmond, North Yorkshire DL11 7EB
Tel: 01833 621218 Fax: 01833 621110

The small village of Barningham lies almost directly on the Durham and North Yorkshire border and has over the years changed its allegiance many times, though for the purpose of this book it shall be deemed to lie on the Durham side of the border! Wilson House can be found between Barningham and Greta Bridge surrounded by some of the most beautiful scenery in England. Located within a large working farm, here you will find comfortable farmhouse bed and breakfast accommodation provided by Helen Lowes. Within the delightful 19th century stone-built house the guest accommodation comprises a double en-suite room with adjoining children's room, a single room and a ground floor en-suite twin room with adjoining single room. All guest rooms have been furnished and maintained to a very high standard and are provided with hot drinks making facilities, colour TV and radio alarm clock. Breakfast, and an evening meal if you would like, is served in the conservatory or dining room and prepared using fresh local and home produced ingredients.

There is also a self-contained cottage adjoining the farmhouse, with its own courtyard, which is available for self-catering holidays. Sleeping up to four people, this is a modern conversion of a disused outbuilding offering a very high standard of accommodation. The two double, en-suite bedrooms are on the ground floor and the kitchen and living room upstairs take advantage of the magnificent views.

DIDDRIDGE FARM

Diddridge Lane, Hamsterley,
Bishop Auckland,
Durham DL13 3PG
Tel: 01388 488520

The charming village of Hamsterley lies to the east of the forest of the same name and here you will find the charming **Diddridge Farm**. This extensive property is built of stone and dates to the early 19th century when it would have been a busy working farm. The grounds extend to 12 acres, including some very fine gardens, and have a tributary of the River Wear running through the centre. Also of interest is the original gin mill - used for the grinding of crops - of round appearance in which a horse would work driving grinding stones. The small room is attached to the former farm outbuildings.

The main farmhouse has been extensively refurbished and updated to provide a comfortable home for owner Sheila Petch. The property is elegantly furnished and carpeted throughout with very stylish decor. Here Sheila is able to offer bed and breakfast accommodation with two comfortable en-suite rooms available. The rooms are warm and comfortable and each are provided with TV and tea and coffee tray. Evening meals can be provided to bed and breakfast guests by prior arrangement. Within the main building there is also a self-contained 4 star holiday apartment, sleeping four, which is available for weekly rental and short breaks (subject to availability).

"Rokeby". The elegant Palladian house, where Scott stayed to write his poem, is open to the public during the summer months.

HAMSTERLEY FOREST
9 miles N of Barnard Castle off the A68

Hamsterley Forest is one of the Forestry Commission's most attractive Forest Parks. This huge area - over 5,500 acres - of mature woodland is managed for timber production, and has 1,100 acres available for recreation with a choice of rides and walks. Today it offers a wide range of activities for visitors, such as informal or guided walks, orienteering, horse-riding and cycling (cycles can be hired). There is a visitor centre with displays on forestry, wildlife and timber usage, and large, grassy areas make splendid picnic spots. The forest is easily accessible from coach and car parks, and visitors are enthusiastically encouraged to enjoy the peace and quiet of this lovely place, which is now a Forest Nature Reserve.

Surprisingly enough, the Forest is largely artificial and relatively recent in origin. Much of it covers areas once worked by the lead-mining industry. It was planted some 40 to 50 years ago with European larch, pine and Norway spruce but, in the clearings, several self-sown species have become established - ash, birch and oak among them - adding variety and colour. This is a good area to discover a range of wild flowers and, in the damper places, fungi. There are still red squirrels as well as roe deer, badgers, adders and up to 40 species of birds including heron, woodcock, sparrow hawk, woodpeckers, fieldfare and goldfinch.

There is always some organised event going on at Hamsterley, be it a night time walk, an afternoon of fun and games for children, or orienteering. A leaflet is available with a timetable.

MIDDLETON-IN-TEESDALE
8 miles NW of Barnard Castle on the B6277

Middleton-in-Teesdale, the capital of Upper Teesdale, is a small, grey town in a dramatically beautiful setting with the Tees running below, while all around is a great backcloth of green hills. The town's links with the lead-mining industry are apparent in the Market Square, where there is a handsome cast-iron fountain which was purchased and placed there in 1877 by the employees of the Quaker-owned London Lead Mining Company. The expense was covered from subscriptions raised for the

River Tees, Teesdale

BRIDGE INN

Bridge Street, Middleton-in-Teesdale,
Durham DL12 0QB
Tel: 01837 640283
Fax: 01837 640283

The charming **Bridge Inn** can be found fronting Bridge Street in the heart of Middleton-in-Teesdale. Built in the mid-18th century the inn has served the local gentry for many years. Part of a long, low, stone built terrace, the cosy interior retains the original stone floors and low beamed ceilings. The general style is simple and uncluttered and this all goes to help create the comfortable ambience you can enjoy here. The Bridge is frequented by the locals and this can generally be taken as a good sign that there is good food and drink to be enjoyed here.

A free house, there is always one or two guest ales on tap which are changed weekly. The bar also stocks a range of beer, lager, spirits and soft drinks. Food is served each lunchtime and evening with the menu offering simple, classic meals and snacks, all home cooked and freshly prepared to order. There is a good choice and vegetarians are also catered for. A games room provides a pool table and the beer garden outside is often used for barbecues in the summer. Live entertainment is arranged with a regular Wednesday quiz and karaoke each Friday night.

THE TEESDALE HOTEL

Market Place, Middleton-in-Teesdale,
Durham DL12 0QG
Tel: 01838 640264 Fax: 01838 640651

In the heart of the charming town of Middleton-in-Teesdale stands the long established **Teesdale Hotel**. Originally a coaching inn, the hotel dates back to the 17th century and is now a listed building retaining its fine stone-built exterior and archway. The character of this lovely building has been retained through the centuries while in recent years the interior has been tastefully modernised to provide a comfortable environment in which to cater to the many customers and residents.

Primarily a country hotel, the property has an English Tourist Board two crown grading . There are 10 en-suite rooms within the main building, all individually furnished, and available in varying sizes from single rooms through to a family room. There are also three self-catering courtyard cottages also comfortably furnished and provided with all the essentials for a holiday away from home. The cottages can sometimes be used for bargain bed and breakfast accommodation subject to availability.

The warm and cosy lounge bar, which is open to residents and non residents, has an open log fire and the traditional decor adds to the relaxing atmosphere. In the courtyard you will find a further bar themed around a Spanish Cantina and Tapas can be enjoyed both here and at the tables outside in the courtyard. There is also a main dining room which provides an ideal setting for elegant dining, with food available from an impressive selection presented by the excellent chefs.

High Force Waterfall

retirement of the company's local superintendent, Robert Bainbridge. At the west end of Hude is **Middleton House**, the company's former headquarters.

Although the lead-mining industry disappeared long ago, Middleton still has the strong feeling of being a mining town, with company-built houses, shops, offices and sober chapels to keep the population suitably moral in outlook. The surrounding hills still bear the scars, with the remains of old workings, spoil-heaps and deep, and often dangerous, shafts. But the town's agricultural links remain strong, with streets still known as Market Place, Horsemarket and Seed Hill. Like Barnard Castle, it is increasing in popularity as a centre from which to explore both Teesdale and the entire North Pennines.

Middleton is also the centre for some magnificent walks in Upper Teesdale. The most famous of these is **The Pennine Way** on its 250-mile route from Derbyshire to Kirk Yetholm in Scotland. It passes through Middleton-in-Teesdale from the south, then turns west along Teesdale, passing flower-rich meadows which turn vivid gold, white and blue in late spring. It then goes past traditional, whitewashed farmsteads and spectacular, riverside scenery, including the thrilling waterfalls at **Low Force**, **High Force** and **Cauldron Snout**.

High Force is beautiful. While it isn't England's highest waterfall, it is its largest in terms of water flow, with the Tees dropping 68 feet over Great Whin Sill. When it's in spate, its rumble can be heard over a mile away. Low Force isn't so much a waterfall as a series of cascades, and is more beautiful, if less spectacular, than its neighbour. Cauldron Spout is a cascade that flows from Cow Green Reservoir, high in the hills, down into the Tees. As the road leaves the course of the River Tees and follows Harwood Beck before Cauldron Snout is reached. However, it can only be visited on foot.

About three miles west of Middleton-in-Teesdale, near the village of **Newbiggin**, is the **Bowlees Visitor Centre**, where information on the area can be obtained. A picnic area and car park have been provided.

ROMALDKIRK
4 miles NW of Barnard Castle on the B6277

Between Middleton and Barnard Castle, the dale becomes less narrow, more intimate and lushly wooded. There are delightful walks close to the river, past the village of Romaldkirk, named after its church dedicated to the little-known

Romaldkirk Countryside

St Romald or Rumwald, son of a Northumbrian king who, miraculously, could speak at birth.

STANHOPE

Stanhope, the capital of Upper Weardale, is a small town of great character and individuality, which still serves the surrounding villages as an important local centre for shops and supplies. It marks the boundary between the softer scenery of lower Weardale and the wilder scenery to the west. The stone cross in the Market Place is the only reminder of a weekly market held in the town by virtue of a 1421 charter. The market continued until Victorian times.

Stanhope enjoyed its greatest period of prosperity in the 18th and 19th centuries when the lead and iron-stone industries were at their height. The town's buildings and architecture reflect this. In an attractive rural setting in the centre of the dale, with a choice of local walks, Stanhope, in its quiet way, is becoming a small tourist centre with pleasant shops and cafés. The town itself is well worth exploring on foot and a useful "walkabout" town trail is available locally or from information centres.

The most dominant building in the Market Square is **Stanhope Castle**, a rambling structure complete with mock-Gothic crenellated towers, galleries and battlements. The building is, in fact, an elaborate folly built by the MP for Gateshead, Cuthbert Rippon in 1798 on the site of a medieval manor house. In 1875 it was enlarged to contain a private collection of mineral displays and stuffed birds for the entertainment of Victorian grouse-shooting parties. In the gardens is the **Durham Dales Centre**.

Stanhope Old Hall, above Stanhope Burn Bridge, is generally accepted to be one of the most impressive buildings in Weardale. This huge, fortified manor house was designed to repel Scottish raiders. The hall itself is part medieval, part Elizabethan and part Jacobean. The outbuildings included a cornmill, a brew house and cattle yards. It is now a hotel.

St Thomas's Church, by the Market Square, has a tower whose base is Norman, and some medieval glass in the west window. In the churchyard you'll find a remarkable fossil tree stump which was discovered in 1962 in a local quarry.

One of the most important Bronze Age archaeological finds ever made in Britain was at **Heathery Burn**, a side valley off Stanhope Burn, when, in 1850, quarrymen cut through the floor of a cave to find a huge hoard of bronze and gold ornaments, amber necklaces, pottery, spearheads, animal bones and parts of chariots. The treasures are now kept in the British Museum.

AROUND STANHOPE

ALLENDALE
14 miles NW of Stanhope on the B6295

Allendale Town lies on the River East Allen, with a backdrop of heather clad

Allen Gorge

moorland, and was once an important centre of the north Pennine lead-mining industry. It retains attractive houses from prosperous times and a surprisingly large number of existing or former inns around the Market Square. A sundial in the churchyard records the fact that the village lies exactly at the mid point between Beachy Head in Sussex and Cape Wrath in Scotland, making it the very centre of Britain.

ALLENHEADS
9 miles NW of Stanhope on the B6295

Allenheads also has lead-mining connections, with its scatter of stone miners' cottages and an irregular village square with pub and chapel in a lovely setting. This is also a centre for fine, upland rambles through the surrounding hills, which still retain many signs of the former industrial activity. From here the main road climbs over Burtree Fell into Weardale, with wild moorland roads branching across to Rookhope to the east and Nenthead to the west.

OAKEY DENE

Allendale, Hexham,
Northumberland NE47 9EL
Tel: 01434 683572

Just a short drive from Allendale Town is the delightful **Oakey Dene** bed and breakfast. This is the private home of Alan and Carol Davison and they extend a warm welcome to their many guests. Dating back to 1823 this was originally a small cottage before being extended to create this fine, large house. The property has been extensively refurbished, retaining many of the original features while creating a

comfortable home. The rural setting is delightful, and the front of the house is covered with a large creeper and other trailing plants while there is also a colourful garden.

Inside, visitors can make use of a sitting room and dining room and the whole of the interior is kept cosy and warm with open log fires that are lit when the weather turns cold. There are three guest bedrooms in all - the double room has an en-suite bathroom, the twin room has a private bathroom and the single room has the use of the bathroom just down the hall.

A delicious home cooked breakfast is served each morning, with home made bread and preserves, and an evening meal can be provided by prior arrangement. Owned and run by a most charming couple, it is clear that they very much enjoy showing off their lovely home and looking after their guests. A real hidden gem.

BLANCHLAND
7 miles N of Stanhope on the B6306

A small, serene estate village on the Northumberland and Durham border. This is another of the area's hidden places, but it's well worth seeking out. Small cottages seem caught in a fold in the hills, and snuggle round a small village square opposite the Lord Crewe Arms.

Killhope Lead Mining Centre

The name of the village gives a clue to its origins, for it is situated on the site of a priory built for the white canons of the Premonstratensian order in 1165. The Lord Crewe Arms, indeed, is housed in the west range of the priory.

COWSHILL
8 miles W of Stanhope on the A689

In a hollow between Cowshill and Nenthead lies Killhope Mine. The Pennines have been worked for their mineral riches, particularly lead, since Roman times but until the 18th century the industry remained relatively primitive and small scale. The development of new techniques of mechanisation in the late 18th and early 19th century allowed the industry to grow until it was second only to coal as a major extractive industry in the

region. Now the country's best-preserved lead-mining site, and designated an ancient monument, Killhope Mine is the focal point of what is now the remarkable **North of England Lead Mining Museum**, dominated by the massive 34-feet high water wheel. It used moorland streams, feeding a small reservoir, to provide power for the lead-ore crushing mills, where the lead-ore from the hillside mines was washed and crushed ready for smelting into pigs of lead.

Much of the machinery has been carefully restored by Durham County Council over recent years, together with part of the smelting mill, underground adits, workshops, a smithy, tools and miner's sleeping quarters.

FROSTERLEY
3 miles E of Stanhope on the A689

The village is famous for Frosterley marble, a black, heavily-fossilised limestone which in former times was extensively used for rich decorative work and ornamentation on great public and private buildings throughout the north. The Chapel of the Nine Altars in Durham Cathedral makes

Killhope Lead Mining Centre

extensive use of this stone, sometimes called "Durham Marble".

IRESHOPEBURN
8 miles W of Stanhope on the A689

At Ireshopeburn, between Cowshill and St John's Chapel, is the delightful little **Weardale Museum**, situated in the former minister's house next to an 18th-century Methodist chapel. The displays include a carefully re-created room in a typical Weardale lead-miner's cottage kitchen, with furnishings and costumes in period. There is a room dedicated to John Wesley, who visited the area on more than one occasion. It is open during the summer months only.

ROOKHOPE
3 miles NE of Stanhope off the A689

Rookhope (pronounced "Rook-up"), in lonely Rookhope Dale, is on the C2C cycle route, and has a history lost in antiquity, going back at least to Roman times.

Rookhope is in one of those hidden North Pennine valleys which richly repay exploration. The remains of lead and iron mine activity, with some gauntly impressive monuments, now blend into quiet rural beauty. The burn shares the valley with the road which eventually climbs past **Rookhope Chimney**, part of a lead-smelting mill where poisonous and metallic-rich fumes were refined in long flues.

Industry of a sort could soon be returning to Rookhope. There are controversial plans to build what could be Europe's largest wind farm near the village.

ST JOHN'S CHAPEL
7 miles W of Stanhope on the A689

St John's Chapel is the capital of Upper Weardale, and was once called St John's

Weardale. Like most of the surrounding villages, it was a lead mining centre and is still the home of an annual Pennine sheep auction in September which attracts farmers from all over the North Pennines. This is the only village in Durham to boast a town hall, a small building in the classical style overlooking the village green. It was built in 1868.

WESTGATE AND EASTGATE
4 miles W of Stanhope on the A689

The area between Westgate and Eastgate was once the Bishop of Durham's deer park, where deer were kept to supply him with venison. The villages are so called because they were the east and west "gates" to this park, with the hunting lodge itself being at Westgate. In 1327 there was nearly a battle on the slopes above Eastgate. Edward II faced a Scottish army there, but the Scots wisely withdrew before fighting could take place.

WOLSINGHAM
5 miles E of Stanhope on the A689

Wolsingham has strong links with the iron and steel industries, the steelworks in the town having being founded by Charles Attwood who was one of the great pioneers in the manufacture of steel. The works once cast a variety of anchors and propellers for ships.

The town is also the home of England's oldest agricultural show, which takes place on the first weekend in September. As with other towns in the area, it hosts a regular farmers' market. The local tourist information centre has dates.

Tunstall Reservoir, north of Wolsingham, and reached by a narrow lane, lies in a valley of ancient oak woods alongside Waskerley Beck. The

HARE AND HOUNDS

24 Front Street, Westgate, Weardale,
County Durham DL13 1RX
Tel: 01388 517212

In the village of Westgate, in the heart of Weardale, the one and only pub is the **Hare and Hounds**. Dating back to 1793 it has always been an ale house and the original stone structure has remained well preserved to this day. Popular both with the locals from the surrounding area, as well as tourists, there is a good sized car park and beer garden to the rear of the property. The pub is also popular with visitors using the many local caravan sites. The establishment has been owned and run by David and Kathleen Nattrass for the past twelve years. David was born in the village and is well liked and respected by his regular customers with whom he has shared many a tale over the years.

The lovely bar area has two open fires with the original fireplaces still in place. The atmosphere is warm and friendly and it would be quite easy to stay longer than you intended! Food is served from a menu offering simple, classic dishes which have all been home cooked and are sensibly priced. The range of bar snacks caters to all tastes, and on Sundays a traditional roast lunch is served. The separate 40-cover function room is available for hire for large groups and private parties and catering can be arranged.

LANDS FARM BED AND BREAKFAST

Westgate-in-Weardale, County Durham DL13 1SN
Tel/Fax: 01388 517210

Just outside the village of Westgate-in-Weardale, on the southern side of the River Wear, you will find the delightful **Lands Farm**. The mixed, working farm extends to over 260 acres and here in the main house Barbara Reed offers traditional farmhouse bed and breakfast. Dating back to the early 19th century the farmhouse has grown and been carefully extended over the centuries and can today be found

surrounded by a clutter of outbuildings giving the whole place a real charm. The main house is attractively painted and decorated with hanging baskets and flowering tubs while inside visitors will find a high standard of comfort throughout.

There are just two letting rooms, each with luxury en-suite facilities, which have been individually decorated and furnished. There is a double room and a family room and each are provided with a colour TV and tea and coffee making facilities. Guests can make use of the comfortable conservatory lounge, which overlooks the attractive gardens, for reading the morning paper, writing postcards or to plan the day's activities. A full English or Continental breakfast, to suit your own taste and appetite, is served each morning in a separate dining room.

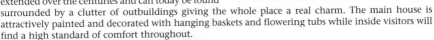

HORSLEY HALL

Eastgate, Bishop Auckland, County
Durham DL13 2LJ
Tel: 01388 517239 Fax: 01388 517608
e-mail hotel@horsleyhall.co.uk
website www.horsleyhall.co.uk

The charming country house hotel of **Horsley Hall**
can be found not far from the village of Eastgate,
on the old road which runs on the south side of
the River Wear. This elegant former manor house
has origins in the 17th century and was once the
home of the Hildyard family, whose connections
with the area go back more than 500 years. In more recent years the property has been carefully
renovated and refurbished while retaining the original character of the building and offering every
convenience for today's guests. The stylish and comfortable accommodation comprises a total of
seven luxurious rooms, each with en-suite bathroom, colour satellite TV, tea and coffee making facilities,

hairdryer and telephone. The restaurant, which is also open to
non-residents, offers a very fine a la carte menu of freshly
prepared dishes which use locally sourced produce wherever
possible. To complement your meal the cellars stock an extensive
wine selection and the friendly and experienced staff are always
available to advise you should you wish.

Surrounding the hall are extensive grounds, which guests
are welcome to explore, incorporating some fine, mature
gardens, a river walk and trout pond. The surrounding area has
much to offer the visitor, with a profusion of places of interest,
areas of natural beauty and interesting towns to visit.

CROSS KEYS

Eastgate, Nr. Stanhope, Durham DL13 2HW
Tel: 01388 517234

The Cross Keys is a charming country inn,
enjoying a prime site within the small village of
Eastgate, just a couple of miles from Stanhope.
The building is thought to date back to 1707 with
some of the outbuildings possibly being even
older. Built of stone, the neat frontage is
decorated with planted flower beds and colourful
hanging baskets. There is also a beer garden with
a stream, which flows through the grounds of
the property, and this is a popular spot in summer months in which to enjoy a cooling drink.

Inside there is a warm and welcoming atmosphere which ensures that regular and first time visitors
feel right at home. The helpful and friendly staff will also go out of their way to ensure that your visit
is a pleasant one. The quality of the food that is served here is one of the main reasons that the Cross

Keys is so busy, attracting local farmers as well those from
further afield who are looking for a special meal out. The
high standard of the cuisine is due in no small part to the
new owner Athol Graham who brings many years experience
as a head chef for a number of well known hotels and also
having previously run a popular establishment in Corbridge.
The menu is outstanding and presents an imaginative
selection of freshly prepared dishes using fresh seasonal and
local produce. The separate restaurant has a stylish and calm
atmosphere and is a delightful setting in which to enjoy
such fine food.

reservoir was built in the mid 19th
century, originally to provide lime-free
water for the locomotives of the
Stockton and Darlington Railway to
prevent their boilers from scaling like a
domestic kettle. It now forms part of a
delightful area to stroll, picnic or go
fishing.

4 Hadrian's Wall and the National Park

This area of West Northumberland, where the North Pennines blend into the Cheviots, is an exhilarating mixture of bleak grandeur, beauty and history. Stretching to the north, towards the Scottish border, are the 398 square miles of the Northumbrian National Park and the Kielder Forest Park, which crosses into Cumbria on the west and into Scotland on the north. To the south is Hadrian's Wall, that monumental feat of Roman civil engineering built on the orders of Emperor Hadrian in AD122.

Towards the east of the area, the hills slope down towards a stretch of fertile land with little towns like Rothbury and Wooler, which in themselves deserve exploration. But up on the high ground a person could walk for miles without meeting another soul. The highest point at 2650 feet is **The Cheviot** itself, a few miles from the Scottish border.

This is the land of the Border reivers, or mosstroopers, bands of marauding men from both sides of the Border who rustled, pillaged and fought among themselves, incurring the wrath of both the English and Scottish kings. A testament to their activities is the fact they gave the word "blackmail" to the English language. The Pennine Way passes over the moorland here, dipping occasionally into surprisingly green and wooded valleys. There are also less strenuous walks circular routes and cycle tracks laid out, with maps and leaflets available from the park visitor centres, at Rothbury, the quaintly-named Once Brewed, and Ingram. Here you can also learn about

The Cheviots in Snow

the history of the area as well as things to see, and - very importantly for a part of the country that can experience severe winter weather - what you should do to enjoy the park in safety.

Three main valleys penetrate the park from the east - **Harthope Valley**, **Breamish Valley** and **Coquetdale**. Harthope Valley is accessed from Wooler, along the Harthope Burn. Part of it is called Happy Valley, and is a popular beauty spot. There are a number of circular walks from the

River Coquet

valley floor up into the hills and back again.

Breamish Valley is the most popular of the valleys, and it's here that the Ingram Visitors Centre, open in the summer months only, is located. Again, there are trails and walkways laid out, with a leaflet available.

Coquetdale is the gentlest of the three, and is popular with anglers. It winds up past Harbottle towards Alwinton and Barrowburn, but in doing so passes through the Otterburn Training Area, where up to 30,000 soldiers a year come to practise their artillery skills. This has actually preserved the upper part of Coquetdale from modern development, and farming here has changed little over the years. There are live firing ranges in the area, so visitors should always heed red danger flags. Plus they should never pick up or handle any device found on the ground, for obvious reasons. The valley is rich in wildlife, and heron, sandpiper and grey wagtail are common. The exposed crags support rock-rose and thyme, and there are patches of ancient woodland.

The Kielder Forest covers 200 square miles, and is to the west of the National Park. It contains Europe's largest man-made lake, Kielder Water, one of Britain's best-used outside leisure assets, opened by the Queen in 1982.

In the south of the National Park is by far the greater part of Hadrian's Wall, the best known Roman monument in Britain, and the best known Roman frontier in Europe. It stretches for 80 Roman miles (73 modern miles) across the country from Bowness-on-Solway in the west to Wallsend in the east, and in 1987 was declared a UNESCO World Heritage Site.

Canoeing in Windy Gyle

From May to September each year **The Hadrian's Wall Bus Service** from Carlisle to Hexham (and Newcastle and Gateshead Metro Centre on a Sunday) goes along the route of the wall, stopping at the main attractions. To see the wall twisting across the moorland is an awe-inspiring site, and no visitor to Northumberland should miss it.

HADRIAN'S WALL AND THE NATIONAL PARK

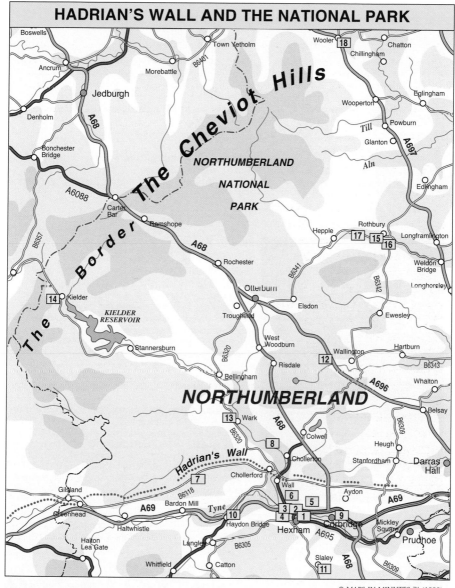

Boswells
Town Yetholm
Wooler 18
Chatton
Chillingham
Ancrum
Morebattle
Eglingham
Jedburgh
Wooperton
Denholm
A68
Powburn
Till
A697
Bonchester
Bridge
Glanton
Aln
The Cheviot Hills
NORTHUMBERLAND
A6088
Edlingham
NATIONAL
Carter
Bar
Ramshope
PARK
Hepple
Rothbury
17 15 16
Longframlington
B6357
A68
Weldon
Bridge
Rochester
B6341
Longhorsley
B6312
14 Kielder
Otterburn
The Border
KIELDER
RESERVOIR
Troughend
Elsdon
Ewesley
The
Stannersburn
West
Woodburn
Hartburn
B6320
Wallington
12
B6343
Risdale
Whalton
Bellingham
A696
NORTHUMBERLAND
Belsay
13 Wark
A68
Colwell
B6309
8
Heugh
B6320
Chollerton
Stanfordham
Darras
Hall
Hadrian's Wall
Chollerford
7
Wall
Aydon
A69
Gilsland
6
B6318
Bardon Mill
3 2 5
A69
Greenhead
A69
Tyne
10
4 1
9
Mickley
Square
Haltwhistle
Haydon Bridge
Hexham
Corbridge
Prudhoe
Halton
Lea Gate
Langley
A695
B6305
Slaley
A68
B6309
Whitfield
Catton
11

PLACES TO STAY, EAT, DRINK AND SHOP

1	Fiona's Bistro, Hexham	Bistro and café	page 66
2	Tap and Spile, Hexham	Pub with food	page 67
3	The Heart of All England, Hexham	Pub with food	page 68
4	The County Hotel, Hexham	Hotel, restaurant & wine bar	page 68

PLACES TO STAY, EAT, DRINK AND SHOP (CONT.)

FIONA'S BISTRO

45 Hallstile Bank, Haugh Lane, Hexham,
Northumberland NE46 3PQ
Tel: 01434 607616

Fiona's Bistro is owned and run by Fiona Anderson who opened the licensed bistro and cafe in the spring of 2000 and has already developed this into a popular little establishment attracting a variety of clientele. Having previously owned a pub and restaurant she has brought plenty of experience to her latest venture and it will undoubtedly do well. Located on the outskirts of Hexham, the situation is convenient for a family meal out, a business lunch or for tourists passing through the area in need of a quick snack.

Open all day, every day, Fiona's offers cooked breakfasts, snacks and full lunches with all meals being home cooked and freshly prepared to order. The menu includes pastas, salads, steak, fish, chicken and vegetarian dishes, with local produce used wherever possible. Chalk boards positioned both outside and on the walls inside offer an additional range of daily specials. The bistro is fully licensed so customers can sample the excellent wine list with their meal.

Fiona's has been created from what was a ground floor storeroom, but the redbrick terrace has been converted into a cosy and intimate bistro. The interior has been stylishly designed and well laid out, comfortably seating up to 20 diners. Fiona's is well worth a visit if you're passing through Hexham.

HEXHAM

Hexham sits in the heart of Tynedale, and is its capital and administrative centre. It's rich in history and character, and sits on a slight terrace above the river. It's famous for **Hexham Abbey**, one of the most important churches in the north of England, and at one time called "the largest and most magnificent church this side of the Alps". It was founded by St Wilfrid in 674, when Queen Etheldreda of Northumbria granted him some land, and the crypt of this early church remains almost intact.

It can be reached by a stairway from the nave, and it is a moving experience to realise that you are in a part of the church that was known to St Wilfrid all these years ago. It was built using Roman stones, and on some of them you can still see inscriptions and carvings.

In 1130 a group of Augustinian canons set up an abbey on the site. The present church dates from the 13th century onwards.

Within the church is an ancient stone chair called the **Frith Stool**, which is 1300 years old. It is said to be that used by St Wilfrid, and may have been a coronation throne for the ancient kings of Northumbria. There is also some wonderful late-medieval architecture, which later restoration has not diminished. It has a rich heritage of carved stone-work, and the early 16th-century rood screen has been described as the best in any monastic church in Britain.

The abbey was sacked many times by the Scots armies who at one time poured over the border into England. However, this was a two way traffic, and the English did likewise to the abbeys at Melrose, Kelso and so on.

TAP AND SPILE

Battlehill, Hexham, Northumberland NE46 1BA
Tel: 01434 602039 Fax: 01434 602039

In the heart of the busy town of Hexham you will find the most delightful hostelry of the **Tap and Spile**. An unprepossessing frontage conceals a characterful, welcoming interior that has been serving the local community since it opened as an ale house in the early 1800s. Popular with the inhabitants of the town and surrounding area, the Tap and Spile is also a convenient refreshment stop for tourists visiting the town. The traditional decor includes local feature photographs and the lounge bar has a wooden floor and exposed stone wall.

Food is served each lunch time and evening with a menu offering a choice of traditional English pub fayre with well-priced dishes catering to all tastes and appetites. To enjoy with a meal, or simply on its own, the bar stocks a good range of beer and lager, as well as the usual wine, spirits and soft drinks, and there is also a selection of real ales kept on tap.

Owned and run by a charming husband and wife team, their lively personalities have contributed greatly to the popularity of this establishment. They also organise a programme of live entertainment with regular folk music, blues nights and live bands.

THE HEART OF ALL ENGLAND

Market Street, Hexham,
Northumberland NE46 3NS
Tel: 01434 603375

The Heart of All England is a charming, characterful inn enjoying a central location within the historic town of Hexham. Dating back to 1833 it is not as old as a majority of the town's buildings, however it has just as delightful an appearance. From the front it looks quite small, an illusion which is quickly dispelled when you walk through the doors! The interior is spacious and open while retaining a cosy, traditional style of decor. This really is a place where anyone, young or old, would feel relaxed and comfortable. Behind the bar they stock a good selection of beer and lager and there is always a choice of real ales on tap.

Food is served from a wide ranging menu offering a choice of snacks, light meals and more hearty options, catering to all tastes and appetites, the portions are of a reasonable size and are well priced. There are occasional theme nights, although the Steak night on a Thursday is a regular fixture. The house special is steak and Guinness pie and this comes heartily recommended. The tenant is Mick Jepps and he proves a charming and humorous host and goes out of his way to make everyone feel relaxed and comfortable.

THE COUNTY HOTEL

Priestpopple, Hexham,
Northumberland NE46 1PS
Tel: 01434 603601 Fax: 01434 603616

Enjoying a prominent location in the town of Hexham, on the unusually named street of Priestpopple, is **The County Hotel**. Dating back to 1837 the building has been much extended over the centuries resulting in an impressive three storey frontage which dominates the surrounding buildings. Built in a classical style the hotel retains the original feature of an impressive revolving front door. The hotel has recently been taken over by Peter and Dianne Harding and the property is undergoing an extensive programme of refurbishment which is due to be completed by April 2001.

This sizeable property incorporates both a restaurant and a wine bar with bistro, each seating up to 40. The cuisine is a classic blend of English and French with the chefs presenting a wide range of dishes, freshly prepared using locally sourced produce. The restaurant boasts both an a la carte and table d'hote menus and is open to both residents and non-residents each lunchtime and evening. Visitors are also welcome to enjoy a drink in the cosy wine bar which is an ideal place to meet up with friends before dinner.

The accommodation comprises a total of 10 en-suite bedrooms of varying sizes. Each room is individually styled and furnished and provided with a colour TV and tea and coffee making facilities to help guests feel right at home. The friendly staff make every effort to ensure that your stay is a pleasant one and will be more than happy to offer advice on day trips and places to visit in the area.

There is much more than the abbey to see in Hexham, however. It overlooks the Market Place, where a lively and colourful market is held each Tuesday. Nearby is the early 14th century **Moot Hall**, built of Roman stone. It was used in olden days as the courtroom of the Archbishop of York, who had the grand title of Lord of the Liberty and Regality

Hexham Abbey

of Hexham. It now houses the **Border History Library**, and also hosts art exhibitions. The **Border History Museum** is housed in the **Manor Office**, which is nearby. This dates from 1330, and was built by the Archbishop as a gaol for his courthouse. It is undoubtedly the oldest purpose-built gaol in the country.

The Border History Museum tells, in a vivid way, the story of the border struggles between Scotland and England. The borderlands were, for many centuries, virtually without rule of law, and ravaged by bands of men called reivers - cattle rustlers and thieves

who took advantage of the disputed border lands. Powerful wardens, or Lords of the Marches - themselves warlords of pitiless ferocity - were given almost complete authority by the king to control the reivers and anyone else who crossed their path. However, for all their power and ferocity they were singularly unsuccessful in controlling the bloodshed. This was the period of the great border ballads, violent and colourful tales of love, death, heroism and betrayal which have found an enduring place in literature.

The town has retained much of its character, with winding lanes and passageways, some delightful shops and a market. There are some attractive 18th and 19th century houses, handsome terraces, delightful gardens around the abbey, and several attractive areas of open space. There are particularly good views, from several points in the town, across the Tyne valley.

Market Street, Hexham

THE RAT INN

Anick, Hexham, Northumberland NE46 4LN
Tel: 01434 602814 Fax: 01434 601099

The unusually named **Rat Inn** enjoys a fabulous elevated site within the small village of Anick, overlooking the town of Hexham and beyond. Looking very much like a private residence it would be easy to drive straight past this hostelry, although its long history going back to 1751 shows that it was originally a drovers inn.

It is quite unique in its decor, is dimly lit to create an intimate ambiance and is much larger than you would think from its outward appearance. Inside there are three large rooms and a separate

restaurant area which looks out over the pretty gardens. The menu offers a surprisingly fine standard of cuisine with a wide selection of dishes on offer, to tantalise every palate and appetite. Freshly prepared, local produce is used wherever possible, all meals are cooked to order and the prices are very reasonable. The bar stocks a wide range of real ales and regular guest ales, all kept in top condition and hand pulled to order.

Outside there is a beer garden and children's play area which are popular in warm weather. The Rat Inn has been run by Donald D'Adamo for many year, and his passion for fine food, combined with his Italian origins, have contributed greatly to the success of this establishment.

THE QUEENS ARMS HOTEL

Main Street, Acomb, Northumberland NE46 4PT
Tel: 01434 602176

Situated in the picturesque Northumberland village of Acomb, two miles North of Hexham and close to the famous Hadrian's Wall, stands **The Queens Arms Hotel**. Dating back to 1908 the inn was built by a local Sea Captain and enjoys a prime site at the top end of the main street. Neatly presented and freshly painted, the property looks very inviting, and those who venture through the doors will not be disappointed. In recent years the property has undergone an extensive programme of refurbishment and now offers bed and breakfast accommodation in four well appointed letting rooms, of which two have full en-suite facilities. Overnight guests can also expect a hearty cooked breakfast in the morning.

In the bar area you will find roaring log fires, superb decor and furnishings which blend traditional features with more modern fittings resulting in a very stylish effect. Customers can enjoy some excellent real ales which are kept in top condition behind the bar, and offered with the usual range of lager, wine, spirits and soft drinks. Food is served from a small menu offering a selection of bar snacks each lunch time. This is a friendly village pub which will appeal to anyone who is looking for a quiet drink.

AROUND HEXHAM

AYDON
4 miles E of Hexham off the B6321

Aydon Castle is a superb example of a Northumbrian fortified manor house or castle, the fortification being necessary in this region in times past to keep the reivers at bay. It dates from the early 14th century, and was built by Robert de Reymes, though there are some later additions. It is often described as one of the best-preserved fortified manor houses in Britain, thanks to its early owners and in more recent years to the efforts of English Heritage.

BARDON MILL
10 miles W of Hexham on the A69

Bardon Mill, a former mining village, stands on the north bank of the South Tyne. An important drovers' road crossed the river here and cattle were fitted with iron shoes at Bardon Mill to help them on their way to southern markets. The village is a convenient starting point for walks along **Hadrian's Wall**. The Roman forts of **Vindolanda** and **Housesteads** are nearby, and both are popular with visitors, having plenty of Roman remains and accompanying exhibitions.

Between Bardon Mill and Haydon Bridge lies the confluence of the South Tyne and the River Allen, which, like the Tyne, comes from two main tributaries - the East Allen and West Allen.

The valleys of the East and West Allen really are hidden jewels. The 22,667 acres of Allen Banks, as the lower part of the valley near the Tyne is known, is a deep, wooded, limestone valley, rich in

MOSS KENNELS FARM
Housesteads, Haydon Bridge, Hexham, Northumberland NE47 6NL
Tel: 01434 344016 Fax: 01434 344016

The Roman fort of Housesteads is a popular tourist attraction on Hadrian's Wall near to Haydon Bridge. Not far from the fort, and enjoying a unrivalled position is the **Moss Kennels Farm**.

This is a working farm, owned and run by Emma Reed and her husband. Dating back to 1842 the main farmhouse is surrounded by 350 acres of land and is approached by a long drive that passes through some most attractive woodland and extensive gardens. The main house is sparsely furnished and yet is cosy and comfortable ensuring that guests feel right at home. The bed and breakfast accommodation is provided in two rooms, both of which are en-suite.

Guests can be guaranteed a hearty farmhouse breakfast in the morning, should they wish, and this will certainly set you up for a day's exploring or sightseeing. An evening meal can be provided by prior arrangement.

The couple have a huge stables and breed and deal in horses, so any guests that are interesting in knowing more, then just ask! This is a remote and stunningly beautiful part of England and it is well worth spending a few days exploring this area. Moss Kennels Farm would make an ideal base.

THE BARRASFORD ARMS HOTEL

Barrasford, Hexham,
Northumberland NE48 4AA
Tel: 01434 681237 Fax: 01434 681237

The village of Barrasford is just five miles north of Hexham and reached just off the A6079 road. Enjoying an elevated position in the heart of the village, **The Barrasford Arms Hotel** has a prime position overlooking the North Tyne river. A traditional village hostelry, this country inn has been in the same family for three generations with the present manager being Tom Milburn, also a local farmer, who runs the place with his wife Joyce. The stone built inn has origins in the late 17th century when it was originally a small cottage, being rebuilt in the 1850s as the well proportioned building you see today. Catering mainly to the surrounding communities this charming inn is well worth a stop if you are travelling and exploring the area.

Joyce masterminds the cooking, producing a simple, fresh menu of delicious dishes using her much loved Aga. Local produce features throughout with the steak being sourced from a local farmer and the ham being home baked. The dining room has some fabulous views over the river and towards Haughton Castle on the opposite bank. Meals and snacks can also be enjoyed in either the public bar or the lounge. Behind the bar there is a choice of beer and lager with a selection of hand-pulled ales also kept on tap. Tom's family have in fact bought their beer from the same supplier for over 70 years though thankfully they no longer have to rely on a horse and cart to transport the barrels up the hill!

Bed and breakfast accommodation can be found here, with a total of five guest rooms available, some en-suite. The family also own self-catering cottages and a camping barn. Ring for full details.

THE DYVELS HOTEL

Station Road, Corbridge, Nr. Hexham,
Northumberland
Tel: 01434 633633
Fax: 01434 632461
e-mail mike@dyvelshotel.co.uk
website www.dyvelshotel.co.uk

Three miles from Hexham, heading out towards Slaley Forest, you may be lucky enough to find **The Dyvels Hotel**. This licensed hotel is as popular for its bar as it is for the comfortable accommodation to be found here, catering to the regular local customers as well as tourists. The charming 18th century building enjoys a remote, rural setting and has an attractive, large beer garden to the front which has a certain splendour even on a frosty winter's day.

The main bar area is most comfortable and the friendly staff offer a relaxed and unhurried service that is popular with customers of all ages, especially those that are in no rush to be somewhere else. Your host, Mike Dodgson, is a local man who has run The Dyvels with his lovely wife for over five years, building a popular reputation with the surrounding community.

In addition to the busy bar the hotel offers a total of five comfortable rooms for bed and breakfast accommodation. Each room has en-suite facilities and is provided with a TV, alarm clock and hot drinks tray. This is an ideal touring base for exploring Hadrian's Wall, the high Durham Dales and Northumberland.

natural beauty, now owned by the National Trust.

BARRASFORD
7 miles N of Hexham off the A6079

Barrasford sits on the North Tyne, across from **Haughton Castle**, of which there are fine views. The castle is one of the finest great houses in Northumberland, and dates originally from the 13th century. Over the succeeding years, additions and alterations have been made, with the west wing being designed by Anthony Salvin and built in 1876. The castle isn't open to the public.

CHOLLERFORD
3 miles north of Hexham on the B6318

The Roman fort of **Chesters**, or Cilurnum, to give it its Roman name, is situated in the parkland created by Nathaniel Clayton round the mansion he had built in 1771. The fort covers nearly six acres and was large enough to accommodate a full cavalry regiment. There is a fine museum with a remarkable collection of Roman antiquities. Remains of the Roman fort include a well-preserved bath house and barracks. Near to the bath house can be

seen the foundations of a Roman bridge that carried a road across the Tyne.

CHOLLERTON
6 miles N of Hexham on the A6079

Chollerton, six miles north of Hexham, enjoys an exceptionally fine setting. Nearby is the site of the **Battle of Heavenfield**, where King (later St) Oswald defeated the army of Cadwalla, a Welsh king. Four miles NW of the village is **Chipchase Castle**, a combination of 14th century tower and Jacobean mansion, open to the public throughout June.

CORBRIDGE
3 miles E of Hexham on the A69

Corbridge is an ancient market town lying snugly in the Tyne valley, and was, for a time, the capital of the ancient Kingdom of Northumbria. The original Roman town, Corstorpitum, lay half a mile to the NW, and the site can be visited. This charming place still retains relics of its former importance as a strategic crossing of the river, including two fortified medieval towers which are evidence of more troubled times. The 14th century **Vicar's Pele** was, as the name implies, formerly the home of the vicar, and the other, **Low Hall**, now forms part of a private house. It dates from the 13th century, with many later additions.

The finest building in Corbridge, however, is **St Andrew's Church**. It still retains many Saxon features, and the base of the tower was once the west porch of the Saxon nave, and within the

Vindolanda Roman Fort

THE ANCHOR HOTEL

John Martin Street, Haydon Bridge, Hexham NE47 6AB
Tel: 01434 684227

Haydon Bridge lies either side of the A69 and was once an important place in the movements of the Scottish and English armies. In the centre of the town is **The Anchor Hotel**, located right on the banks of the river. The first reference to an inn on this site goes back to 1422 when a certain John Parker was hanged in the courtyard for felony. In 1528, in a letter from the Earl of Northumberland to Cardinal Wolsey, there is reference to another hanging. Another part of the Anchor originally formed a courthouse of the 'leet and court baron of the barony of Langley' and records of court proceedings go back to 1630. Langley Castle, now beautifully restored and privately owned, is just two miles away. By the time of the Jacobite rebellion in 1715 the Admiral's House was built and now forms part of the hotel. The Anchor subsequently became an important and busy Coaching Inn, being midway between Newcastle and Carlisle and was the original meeting place for the Haydon Hunt, formed in 1812, and understood to be the oldest hunt in Northumberland.

Now a substantial riverside hotel there are some unbeatable views over the surrounding countryside and of the fast flowing River Tyne. Recently taken over by Joyce Coates, this is a popular place to stay and the location is ideal as a base for exploring this picturesque area. The cosy Restaurant overlooks the river and bridge, which gives the town its name, and the menu offers a superb choice of fine dishes. The new chef utilises fresh local produce where possible and the steaks are the house speciality. There is also a public bar, lounge and separate function suite, available for private hire and small parties. Regular entertainment is arranged with live acoustic sessions and pub quizzes. The accommodation comprises a total of 12 en-suite rooms with two being on the ground floor and fully accessible for the disabled. Each room is individually furnished and all have stunning views.

RYE HILL FARM

Slaley, Nr. Hexham, Northumberland NE47 0AH
Tel: 01434 673259 Fax: 01434 673259
e-mail enquiries@consult.courage.co.uk
website www.ryehillfarm.co.uk

Rye Hill Farm has a history going back 300 years and is a traditional, stone built Northumbrian farmhouse surrounded by 30 acres of privately owned land. This is a small working farm which has a few pigs, sheep, poultry and ponies and visitors can enjoy a unique opportunity to see what goes on each day. The surrounding countryside is criss-crossed by a network of footpaths which lead into the forests, along the river or onto the nearby moorland.

The cosy farmhouse and adjoining buildings has been adapted to provide both bed and breakfast and self-catering accommodation and well behaved children and dogs are welcome by arrangement. There are a total of six en-suite rooms for bed and breakfast of varying sizes. Overnight guests have their own dining room where a traditional cooked breakfast is served each morning and an evening meal can be provided on request. The self-catering accommodation can sleep up to nine in four bedrooms. The ground floor is suitable for wheelchair access and the twin en-suite room incorporates a walk-in shower. Available for week long lets throughout the year. All guests can all enjoy use of the games room, utility room and DIY laundry facilities. Caravans and campers can also be accommodated within the farm's grounds - ring for details.

Chesters Roman Fort

tower wall is a complete Roman arch, no doubt removed from Corstorpitum at some time.

Corbridge is the site of the **Northumberland County Show**, held on the late May Bank Holiday Monday each year.

HALTWHISTLE
15 miles W of Hexham on the A69

Haltwhistle owes its name, not to the coming of the railway, but to the Saxon words "haut wiscle", meaning "junction of streams by a hill". It is difficult to imagine that this pleasant little town with its grey terraces was once a mining area, but evidence of the local industries remain. An old pele tower is incorporated into the Red Lion Hotel in the town centre. **Holy Cross Church**, behind the Market Place, dates back to the 13th century and is said to be on the site of a church founded by William the Lion, King of Scotland in 1178, when this area formed part of Scotland.

Twelve miles NW of Haltwhistle, off the B6318, is **Walltown Quarry**, a recreation site built where an old quarry once stood, and part of the

Northumberland National Park. Trails, including one for orienteering, have been laid out, and the visitor can see the oystercatcher, curlew, sandpiper and lapwing.

HAYDON BRIDGE
6 miles W of Hexham on the A69

Two bridges cross the Tyne here - a modern concrete one dating from 1970, and an older one dating from 1776. North of the village is **Haydon Old Church**, close to where the medieval village of Haydon lay. It dates partly from the 12th century.

LANGLEY
6 miles W of Hexham on the B6295

Langley Castle, now a hotel, is a massive keep built around 1350. In 1450, Henry 1V had it destroyed, but it was restored in the 1890s by a local historian, Cadwallader Bates. In the 17th and early 18th centuries it was owned by the Earls of Derwentwater, and in 1716 the third earl, James, was beheaded in London for his part in the 1715 Jacobite rebellion. His brother Charles was later beheaded for his part in the 1745 uprising. A memorial to them sits beside the A686 not far from the castle.

SLALEY
4 miles SE of Hexham, off the B6306

Slaley is a quiet village consisting of one long street with some picturesque houses dating from the 17th, 18th and 19th centuries. Opposite the 19th century **St Mary's Church** is one of the

CORNHILLS GUEST HOUSE

Kirkwhelpington, Northumberland,
Northumberland NE19 2RE
Tel: 01830 540232
Fax: 01830 540388
e-mail cornhills@farming.co.uk
web: www.northumberlandfarmhouse.co.uk

Enjoying a rural location in the heart of
Northumberland, Cornhills Guest House can be
found near to the village of Kirkwhelpington,
just off the A696 Newcastle to Otterburn road.
This working farm is a perfect base for a touring
holiday in the area with the National Park,
Wallington House, Belsay Castle and Cragside
almost on the doorstep.

This charming house was built in 1888 by the family of the present owners and stands in one acre
of delightful gardens. The large lawn is beautifully maintained, bordered by shrubs, roses and fruit
trees, and a gravel drive leads to the front door while to the rear of the property there is a car park.

Visitors to Cornhills will find the interior equally appealing being attractively decorated and
furnished throughout in keeping with the period of the house. The large downstairs reception rooms
boast high ceilings, with a mosaic hall floor leading to an elegant lounge with marble fireplace. A
Canadian pine staircase leads upstairs to the three comfortable guest rooms, two with an en-suite
bathroom while the third enjoys separate, private facilities. Guests can enjoy a home-cooked traditional
breakfast in the morning while evening meals are available by prior arrangement to guests staying
more than one night. Many of the rooms enjoy spectacular views over the surrounding countryside
which contribute to making this one of the nicest guest houses you are likely to find.

finest - Church View. **Slaley Hall**, two
miles to the SW, has some interesting
gardens.

White Chapel, nr Slaley

OTTERBURN

The village of Otterburn stands almost
in the centre of the National Park, in the
broad valley of the River Rede. It makes
an ideal base for exploring the
surrounding
countryside, an
exhilarating area of open
moorland and rounded
hills. It was close to
here, on a site marked by
the 18th century **Percy
Cross**, that the **Battle of
Otterburn** took place in
1388 between the
English and the Scots.

But it wasn't a full
scale battle as such, and
it might have remained
relatively obscure if it
wasn't for the number of

ballads it spawned - everything from the English "Chevy Chase" to the Scottish "Battle of Otterburn". By all accounts it was a ferocious encounter, even by the standards of the day, and one commentator said that it "was one of the sorest and best fought, without cowards or faint hearts".

A gathering of Scottish troops at Jedburgh in 1388 had resolved to enter England in a two pronged attack - one towards Carlisle and one down into Redesdale. In charge of the Redesdale contingent was the Earl of Douglas, and he got as far as Durham before being harried back to the border by Henry Percy, better known as "Hotspur", and his brother Ralph.

In August the English caught up with the Scottish army at Otterburn, and went straight into attack. It continued for many hours, gradually descending into a series of hand to hand fights between individual soldiers. Gradually the Scots got the upper hand, and captured both Percys. But it was a hollow victory, as the Earl of Douglas was killed. A second force under the Bishop of Durham hurried north when it heard the news, but it wisely decided not to engage in battle. A series of markers known as "Golden Pots" are said to mark the journey of Douglas's body when it was taken back to Melrose.

Otterburn Mill dates from the 18th century, though a mill is thought to have stood on the site from at least the 15th century. Although production of woollens ceased in 1976, the mill is still open, and on display are Europe's only original working "tenterhooks" (hence the expression, "being on tenterhooks"), where newly woven cloth was stretched and dried.

There are some interesting walks round Otterburn, and on some of the surrounding hills can be seen the remains of Iron Age forts. The ones on Fawdon Hill and Colwell Hill are probably the best preserved.

North of the village are the remains of **Brementium** Roman fort. It was first built by Julius Agricola in the 1st century, though what the visitor sees now is mainly 3rd century. It could hold up to 1000 men, and was one of the defences along the Roman road now known as Dere Street. And close by is the **Brigantium Archaeological Reconstruction Centre**, where you can see a stone circle of 4000BC, Iron Age defences, cup and ring carvings and a section of Roman road.

AROUND OTTERBURN

BELLINGHAM AND WARK
7 miles SW of Otterburn on the B6320

The North Tyne is fed by the Kielder Water and, on its way down to join the South Tyne above Hexham, passes two interesting villages, Bellingham and Wark.

Bellingham (pronounced "Bellin-jam") is actually a small market town in a moorland setting, with a broad main street and market place, and an austere little **St Cuthbert's Church**, reflecting the constant troubles of the area in medieval times. To prevent marauding Scots from burning it down, a massive stone roof was added in the early 17th century.

In the churchyard at Bellingham, an oddly-shaped tombstone somewhat reminiscent of a peddler's pack is associated with a foiled robbery attempt that took place in 1723. A peddler arrived at Lee Hall, a mansion once situated between Bellingham and Wark, and asked if he could be put up for the

The Battlesteads Hotel

Wark, Hexham, Northumberland NE48 3LS
Tel: 01434 230209 Fax: 01434 230730
e-mail info@battlesteads-hotel.co.uk website www.battlesteads-hotel.co.uk

It is thought that much of the village of Wark was built of stone taken from Hadrian's Wall, which would go some way to explain why many of the buildings have the same colouring. **The Battlesteads Hotel** is probably no exception, though it is known that it was originally a farmhouse built in the 17th century. Over the years the building has been much extended resulting in the impressive establishment you find today. In more recent times the property has been carefully refurbished and updated to ensure that today's customers find comfortable surroundings in which to rest a while, enjoy a drink or a bite to eat. The interior, which comprises a bar, lounge and restaurant, is superbly furnished throughout with careful attention having been paid to every detail. The attractive Lindisfarne

restaurant is open every evening and provides a delightfully intimate setting in which to enjoy an exceptional, table d'hote meal. The menu features local produce with a wide selection of meat, fish and vegetarian dishes to choose from. To round off your lovely meal there is also a tempting choice of desserts.

The accommodation comprises a total of 14, elegant en-suite rooms, available in varying sizes, including some family rooms. All have a colour TV, hot drinks tray, hair dryer, trouser press and ironing board. The high standard of the accommodation has led to The Battlesteads Hotel being awarded the title of National Small Hotel of the Year 2000.

night. As her master was away at the time the maid refused, but said that he could leave his heavy pack at the Hall and collect it the next day.

Imagine her consternation when some time later the pack began to move. Hearing her screams for help, a servant rushed to the scene and fired his gun at the moving bundle. When blood poured out and the body of an armed man was discovered inside, the servants realised that this had been a clever attempt to burgle the Hall. They sounded a horn which they found inside the pack next to the body, and when the robber's accomplices came running in response to the prearranged signal, they were speedily dealt with.

Wark is to the south of Bellingham, and is an attractive estate village, once part of the lordship of Wark. The Scottish kings are said to have held court here in the 12th century.

On the slopes overlooking the North Tyne are a large number of prehistoric settlements, many of them with picturesque names such as Male Knock Camp, Good Wife Camp, Nigh Folds Camp, Carryhouse Camp and Shieldence Camp.

BRANXTON
26 miles N of Otterburn off the A697

The site of the famous **Battle of Flodden Field** can be found near Branxton, marked by a cross in a cornfield reached by a short path. It was here that the English army heavily defeated a Scottish army under the command of King James IV on 9th September 1513. The king was killed, and his body lay in **St Paul's Church** in Branxton, now rebuilt. A discreetly positioned car park is provided on the

Branxton Church

some of the worst border fighting. In later years it became an important stopping point on the drovers' road.

In the late 19th century, when the church was being restored, over 1000 skulls were uncovered. They are though to be those of soldiers killed at the Battle of Otterburn.

Elsdon Tower, which in 1415 was referred to as the "vicar's pele", dates from the 14th century, though it was largely rebuilt at a later date. It is one of the most important pele towers of the region and is now a private residence.

road and there is an information board which explains the background to the battle and how it was fought. A booklet can be purchased at St Paul's Church.

ELSDON
3 miles E of Otterburn on the B6341

The village of Elsdon is of great historical importance. Built around a wide green, with **St Cuthbert's Church** in the middle, it was the medieval capital of Redesdale - the most lawless place in Northumberland, and scene of

HEPPLE
8 miles NE of Otterburn on the B6341

Hepple has a reminder of the difficulty of life near the borders in the form of **Hepple Tower**, a 14th-century pele tower built so strongly that attempts to demolish it and use the stone for a new farmhouse had to be abandoned. West of the village, on the moors, are some fine examples of fortified houses and farms.

KIELDER
16 miles W of Otterburn off the B6320

Kielder village was built in the 1950s to house workers in the man-made **Kielder Forest**, which covers 200 square miles to west of the Northumberland National Park. Initially the planting of the trees brought employment to this area, and families came here from Tyneside and beyond for work and a home. Technology has since taken over and very few workers are now employed.

Here at Kielder Forest you'll find one of the few areas in Britain that contains more red squirrels than grey ones, and an area that abounds with deer and rare

The Walls, Elsdon Church

THE ANGLERS ARMS

Kielder, Northumberland NE48 1AR
Tel: 01434 250072 e-mail anglers.arms@barbox.net

Within the village of Kielder, at the head of Kielder Water, you will find **The Anglers Arms** public house. Built in the early 1980s, at the same time as the reservoir itself, this pub is built in the style of a mountain retreat, and enjoys a quiet setting surrounded by woodland. The open bar area has a large window making it bright and airy, and there is also a separate function room available for private hire and a games room with pool table. Although the style of the building is very modern, its remote location gives it a certain charm.

The surrounding grounds, large beer garden, and pets corner mean that younger customers can be well occupied without getting under their parent's feet. There is a strong emphasis on the serving of

good quality food, here at the Anglers Arms, with the menu offering a tempting range of, reasonably priced, traditional home-cooked dishes catering to all tastes and appetites. There are regular lunch time specials, plenty of vegetarian choices and the menus, which are regularly updated to make the most of seasonal and local produce, are displayed on blackboards hanging on each wall. Good disabled access.

birds. Rare plants also grow here, and there's some excellent walking to be had. There are routes to suit all abilities, from a leisurely stroll to an energetic climb, with maps and leaflets to guide you round. There are also cycle routes, including the 17 mile Kielder Water Cycle Route, and bicycles can be hired from the local visitors centre.

Within the forest is **Kielder Water**, opened by the Queen in 1982, and the largest man-made lake in Northern Europe. It has 27 miles of shoreline, and there's an art and sculpture trail laid out in the forest round its shores. The visitor can even take a pleasure cruise aboard the Osprey, an 80 seat passenger cruiser.

To the north west is **Kielder Castle**, at one time a hunting lodge for the Duke of Northumberland, and later offices for the Forestry Commission. It is now a fascinating visitor centre with exhibits describing the development of the

forest, and an exhibition on the birds of Kielder.

KIRKNEWTON
24 miles NE of Otterburn on the B6351

Kirknewton is a typical border village of cottages, school and village church. In its churchyard is buried **Josephine Butler**, the great Victorian social reformer and fighter for women's rights, who retired to Northumberland and died here in 1906. Her father had been a wealthy landowner, and a cousin of British prime minister Earl Grey of Howick Hall, near Craster. **St Gregory's Church** dates mainly from the 19th century, though there are medieval fragments. It contains an unusual medieval sculpture which shows the Magi wearing kilts - a fascinating example of medieval artists presenting the Christian story in ways their audience could understand.

Upper Coquet, Cheviot Hills

ROTHBURY
12 miles E of Otterburn on the B6341

Rothbury is a natural focal point from which to explore the valley of the River Coquet. It is an excellent starting point for some delightful walks along the valley or through the nearby woodland, the most famous perhaps being to the **Rothbury Terraces**, a series of parallel tracks along the hillside above the town, or **Simonside**, a hill offering a fine viewpoint.

Simonside is a hill steeped in history.

Half a mile east of the village, in what are now fields by the little River Glen, once lay the royal township of Gefrin or Ad-Gefrin, better known as **Yeavering**. It was discovered in 1948 through aerial photography, and this was where King Edwin of Northumbria built a huge palace of wood in the 7th century that included a royal hall over 100 feet long, storehouses, stables, chapels and living quarters. A stone, and a board explaining the layout, now marks the place where this long-vanished royal establishment once stood.

Cragside Country Park

If such historical associations were not enough, on the summit of a nearby hill known as **Yeavering Bell**, there is a magnificent Iron-Age hill fort, the largest in Northumberland, enclosed by the remains of a thick wall and covering 13 acres. Over 130 hut circles and similar buildings have been traced on the summit, which commands impressive views for miles around.

Flint arrowheads have been recovered there, as well as bronze swords, shards of pottery, axe heads and ornaments. Burial cairns abound, as do carved stones and ancient paths. The Northumberland National Park has prepared a leaflet which guides you on a walk up and onto the hill.

To the north of Simonside is **Lordenshaws**, another landscape full of history and atmosphere. There's a well-

THE SUN KITCHEN

High Street, Rothbury, Northumberland NE65 7TJ
Tel: 01669 620629 Fax: 01669 620629
e-mail chris.alborough@1c24.net

At the top end of the small town of Rothbury, visitors will find **The Sun Kitchen**. This cosy establishment is a traditional tea shop, owned and run by Enid and Chris Alborough , and together they have created a warm and friendly environment. Open nearly every day, here you can enjoy morning coffee, lunch and afternoon tea, and choose from the very varied selection of home made scones, cakes and tarts that are always available. All the portions are of a good size and very reasonably priced and the hot lunches would definitely appeal to those with a hearty appetite! The interior is light and airy and can seat up to 30 diners with the tables all well spaced to avoid bumping elbows with your neighbour.

The building in which The Sun Kitchen is housed dates back to 1778 when it was built as a coaching house. The structure is of the local stone and is positioned adjoining a small attractive mews development. The frontage is neatly kept and freshly painted and in summer shows the window boxes and planted tubs at their best. This is a convenient stop en-route to Cragside which would provide a fascinating day out for all the family.

KATERINA'S GUEST HOUSE

Sun Buildings, High Street, Rothbury, Northumberland NE65 7TQ
Tel: 01669 620691

The village of Rothbury would make a ideal base for a touring holiday or short break, and where better to stay than at **Katerina's Guest House**, right in the centre of the village. The property dates back to the 17th century when it once formed part of the 'Old Sun' coaching inn, and the building retains much of the original charm and character.

Previous visitors to Rothbury may recall that this was once Katerina's Restaurant, a popular eating place which was noted for the quality of its food and cosy atmosphere. Owned by the same couple, the property has since been converted to provide three cosy guest rooms, each with modern en-suite facilities to ensure a comfortable stay. Each room has been individually furnished and decorated to complement the original features of stone fireplaces and beamed ceilings. Visitors of all ages and interests are welcome though each room has a four poster bed making it perfect for romantic couples!

Guests can enjoy a wide choice at breakfast, with the traditional cooked English breakfast being offered together with a selection of yoghurt, home-baked bread, continental meats, and the owners favourite - Scotch Whisky porridge. Evening meals are available by arrangement, and again you can expect a very high standard of cuisine. The house speciality is Steak Katerina and the home-made meringues are out of this world!

Owned and personally run by Cathryn and Ian Mills, this is a cosy and friendly establishment, run by a lovely couple who enjoy making their guests feel right at home.

Cragside Estate

a natural marketplace for Upper Coquetdale, to which cattle and sheep were brought for sale and the drovers provided with numerous alehouses. Since the mid 19th century Rothbury has been a holiday resort for walkers and fishermen, and the railway, which opened in 1870, contributed further to its growth. It is now popular with retired people and commuters to Morpeth and Newcastle.

defined hill fort, Bronze Age burial mounds, rock carvings and cairns. Again, a leaflet is available.

Rothbury has Saxon origins, and the church is an ancient foundation though almost entirely rebuilt in 1850. From the 18th century the village developed into

Just outside Rothbury is the house and estate of **Cragside**, once the home of Sir William Armstrong, arms manufacturer and industrialist. He bought 14,000 acres in the valley of the Debden Burn, and employed architect Norman Shaw to extend the existing house and make it

THE CROSS KEYS

Thropton, nr Rothbury, Morpeth,
Northumberland NE65 7HX
Tel: 01669 620362

Situated a couple of miles from Rothbury, travelling towards Otterburn on the B6341, is the pretty village of Thropton, a journey well worth making for here you will find **The Cross Keys Inn**. This fine country hostelry dates back to the early-19th century and is built of the local stone, though the frontage is hard to see clearly as it is covered with a sprawling red creeper. The building enjoys an elevated position, slightly higher than the rest of the village, and has some fine views. The inn has a warm, welcoming atmosphere and serves a wide variety of fine ales and food of

a very high standard which are regularly enjoyed by both the locals and visitors to the area. The cosy interior is kept warm and inviting in cooler months by the open fires. Food is served each lunch time and evening from a varied menu catering to all tastes and at very reasonable prices. Recently taken over by a delightful couple, George Yule and Gale Hooper, they have brought new life and some fresh ideas to the place. George is a trained chef and Gale has lots of experience in working behind a bar, so there could well be some changes in the years to come.

Should you wish to stay in the area longer, bed and breakfast accommodation is available throughout the year. There are four bedrooms furnished to a high standard, each being equipped with a TV and tea and coffee making facilities, and they share a bathroom. Reasonable rates.

suitable to entertain royalty and other wealthy guests. Work began in 1864, and what finally emerged in 1884 was a mock Tudor Victorian mansion. A pioneer of the turbine, Armstrong designed various pieces of apparatus for the house, and devised his own hydroelectric systems, with man-made lakes, streams and miles of underground piping, making Cragside the first house in the world to be lit by hydroelectricity. The house is now owned by the National Trust, and restored sympathically to show how upper middle class Victorians were beginning to combine comfort, opulence and all the latest technology in their homes

WELDON BRIDGE

15 miles E of Otterburn on the A697

Weldon Bridge is an exceptionally elegant bridge across the River Coquet,

dating from 1744. Although it no longer carries the main road it remains an impressive feature.

Nearby is **Brinkburn Priory**, standing in secluded woodland on the banks of the river. It was established in about 1135 by William de Bertram, 1st Baron Mitford, and is thought to have been built by the same masons who constructed nearby Longframlington church. It is in a beautiful setting surrounded by ancient trees and rhododendrons and was once painted by Turner as a romantic ruin. Its church was restored in 1859 by Thomas Austin on behalf of the Cadogan family, and has many fine architectural features.

WOOLER

22 miles NE of Otterburn on the A697

Wooler is a small town standing on the northern edge of the Cheviots, midway between Newcastle and Edinburgh, and

THE RED LION

1 High Street, Wooler,
Northumberland NE71 6LD
Tel: 01668 281629

In the heart of the small town of Wooler you will find at one end of the High Street, **The Red Lion**. This long established hostelry dates back to the late 1500s when it was built to serve the residents of the town as well as the many travellers along the busy road between Coldstream and Newcastle. Wooler suffered from a number of fires in centuries past due to the large number of buildings at one time having thatched

roofs. Thankfully the Red Lion survived the largest of the fires in 1863 which destroyed most of the High Street. Within two years most of the buildings were rebuilt, with tiled roofs!

A large, solid building, The Red Lion is built of local materials and features some fine stone mullioned windows. Inside visitors will find bright, warm, drinking areas with a long and well stocked bar. A neat little restaurant area seats just 20, though meals and snacks can be taken in the lounge bar. Food is served from a small, yet well balanced menu offering a choice of classic, tasty dishes. Meals are freshly prepared to order and are reasonably priced. This is a family run establishment, and it is the owner herself, Mildred Crossman, who ensures that food is prepared to the highest of standards and makes sure that no one will leave hungry.

If you are in need of somewhere to stay there is also bed and breakfast accommodation available, with four en-suite guest rooms.

is an excellent centre for exploring both the Cheviots and the border country. In the 18th and early 19th centuries it became an important halt on the main north-south coaching route and is now a small market town where many cattle fairs once took place.

There are no outstanding buildings in Wooler, though the town itself makes a pleasing whole. There are superb walking opportunities from its outskirts to, for example, the Iron Age hill fort immediately west of the town - an impressive viewpoint - or to **Earle Whin** and **Wooler Common,** or via Harthope onto The Cheviot itself. Alternatively, the visitor can take a vehicle into the Harthope Valley with a choice of walks, easy or strenuous, up and through the magnificent hillsides of this part of the Northumberland National Park.

The visitor can also climb **Humbledon Hill**, on top of which are the remains of a hill fort, built about 300BC. The Battle of Humbledon Hill

was fought here in 1402 between the English and the Scots, who had been on a raiding mission as far south as Newcastle. Due to the firepower of Welsh bowmen in the English army, the Scottish army assembled within the fort was easily defeated. Human and horse bones have been uncovered while ploughing the hill's northern slopes, and there is an area still known to this day as Red Riggs from the blood which stained the ground during and after the battle.

WOOPERTON
20 miles NE of Otterburn off the A697

Wooperton is close to the site of the **Battle of Hedgeley Moor** which took place in 1464. In truth this was more of a skirmish, in which the Yorkist Lord Montague defeated the Lancastrian Sir Ralph Percy, who was killed. The site is marked by a carved stone called the **Percy Cross** and can be reached along a short footpath leading from the A697.

5 The Northumberland Coastal Area

The area from the edge of the Cheviots to the coast, and from Berwick-upon-Tweed in the north to the River Blyth in the south, is predominantly rural, though there is some bleak moorland as well as some industry around the south east. This is an area of quiet villages and small towns, with the exception of Ashington, which has a population of 25,000.

Ross Back Sands

Here you'll find what most people consider to be the finest coastline in England - that stretch that goes from the Scottish border above Berwick down to Cresswell, a distance of 40 miles. It's been designated as the North Northumberland Heritage Coast, and takes in such historical places as Bamburgh Castle, Lindisfarne, the Farne Islands and Dunstanburgh Castle.

For all its beauty, it's a quiet coastline, and you can walk for miles along the dunes and beaches without meeting another soul. No deck chairs or chiming ice cream vans here - just a quietness broken occasionally by the screeching of gulls. At Cocklawburn, just south of Berwick, you'll find fossil beds, and Coquet Island is a renowned bird sanctuary where the visitor can see puffins, roseate terns, razorbills, cormorants and eiders.

Alnnwick Castle

But perhaps the most

Nesting Birds, Farne Islands

evocative place of all on the coast is Lindisfarne, a small island lying between Bamburgh and Berwick. It was to here that St Aidan and a small community of Irish monks came from Iona in AD635 to found a monastery from which missionaries set out to convert northern England to Christianity. And it was on Inner Farne that St Cuthbert, Bishop of Lindisfarne, lived an austere and simple life.

Inland from the coast the land is heavily farmed, and there is a pleasant landscape of fields, woodland, country lanes and farms. The villages are especially fine, most with their ancient parish churches and village greens. The green was essential in olden times, as the Scots constantly harried this area, and the villagers needed somewhere to guard their cattle after bringing them in from the surrounding land.

This being so, it's also a land of castles, such as Norham, Etal, Chillingham and Edlingham. Some have been converted into grand mansions for the great families of the area, while others are now no more than ruins.

The area to the south east, around Ashington, was once coalmining country, though the scars are gradually being swept away. But at Woodhorn the industry is remembered in a museum of mining. Even here, however, an

Lindisfarne (Holy Island)

earlier history is evident, as the former Woodhorn church is one of the most interesting in Northumberland.

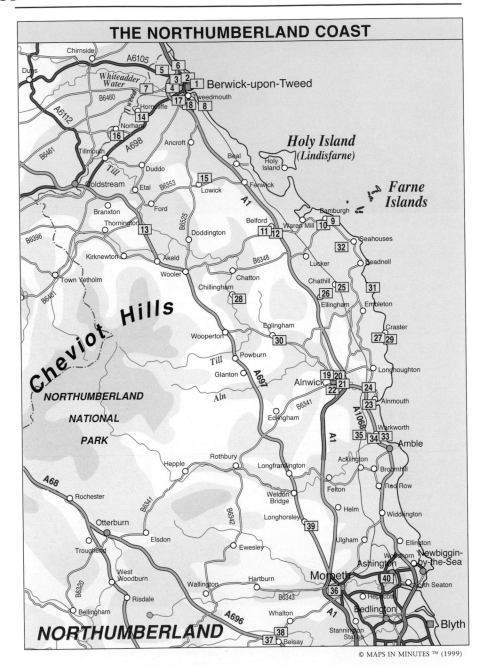

THE NORTHUMBERLAND COAST

© MAPS IN MINUTES ™ (1999)

PLACES TO STAY, EAT, DRINK AND SHOP

QUEENS HEAD HOTEL

Sandgate, Berwick-upon-Tweed,
Northumberland TD15 1EP
Tel: 01289 307852 Fax: 01289 307858

The magnificent **Queens Head Hotel** dates back to 1820 and is situated within a terrace of buildings, near the centre of Berwick. Renowned for its warm and friendly atmosphere, this small and cosy hotel offers its guests the choice of six bedrooms all provided with en-suite facilities, colour TV and complimentary tea and coffee maker. The Queens Head Hotel has been personally run by Pat Kerr for over 16 years, in fact she loved this beautiful old building so much that when it became available to buy five years ago, she decided to purchase it and run it as her own. The hotel has become so well liked that many visitors return time and time again.

The beamed restaurant enjoys a relaxed and welcoming atmosphere and is the perfect place to sit and peruse the comprehensive menu while enjoying a glass of wine from the varied wine list. The chef uses only the freshest local ingredients to produce the delicious dishes that appear on the regularly changing menu. You will also be able to enjoy a fine pint of real ale at the Queens, with a selection always on tap. The Hotel is ideally situated for the visitor, being just minutes from the sea, the river, golf course and the many other amenities that this town has to offer. Pets welcome by prior arrangement.

ALANNAH GUEST HOUSE

84 Church Street, Berwick-upon-Tweed,
Northumberland TD15 1DU
Tel: 01289 307252 Fax: 01289 307252
e-mail: eileenandian@alannahhouse.freeserve.co.uk
website: www.alannahhouse.co.uk

In a quiet corner of Berwick, not far from the town's barracks, you will find **Alannah Guest House**. Dating back to 1706, the Georgian house was originally a Church Manse and was also once used by the barracks as officers' married quarters. The present owner Eileen Sutherland has been here for over 25 years and is responsible for much of the renovation and refurbishment

that has been carried out to maintain some of the historic character of the building. The house is also kept beautifully decorated throughout to make it as comfortable and homely as possible while providing everything guests may require resulting in Alannah House having an English Tourist Board Four Diamonds Highly Commended rating.

Accommodation is available in three rooms - a family room, a double and a twin. All the rooms have an en-suite shower room and are provided with a TV and tea and coffee making tray. Guests are also offered use of a washing machine and ironing facilities. A choice of cooked breakfasts are served and evening meals are available by arrangement. Alannah House is within two minutes walk of the main shopping area and there is plenty to see and do within the town. The bus and rail stations are also not far away.

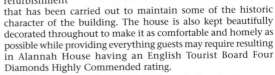

BERWICK-UPON-TWEED

Along part of its length, the River Tweed serves as the border between Scotland and Northumberland. But a few miles to the west of Berwick, the border takes a curious lurch north, and curls up and over the town to the east before reaching the coast. So, while Berwick is on the north bank of the Tweed, it's well and truly within Northumberland.

For centuries, the town was fought over by the Scots and the English, and changed hands no less than 14 times until it finally became part of England in 1482. But even now, Scotland exerts a great influence. The local football team, Berwick Rangers, plays in the Scottish League, and in 1958 the Lord Lyon, who decides on all matters armorial in Scotland, granted the town a coat-of-arms - the only instance of armorial bearings being granted in Scotland for use in England.

But for many years after becoming English, the town was a curious anomaly. It was declared a "free burgh", a situation that lasted in one form or another right up until 1885. When war was declared on Russia in 1853, it was done in the name of "Victoria, Queen of Great Britain, Ireland, Berwick-upon-Tweed and all the British Dominions". When peace was announced in 1856, no mention was made of Berwick. So technically, the town remained at war with Russia.

The situation was rectified in 1966, when a Soviet official made a goodwill visit to the town, and a peace treaty was signed. During the ceremony, the Berwick mayor told the Soviet official that the people of Russia could at last sleep easy in their beds.

Berwick's original medieval walls were built in the 13th century by Edward I.

They were subsequently strengthened by Robert the Bruce when he recaptured the town in 1318, and finally rebuilt by Italian engineers at the behest of Elizabeth I between 1558 and 1569, though the work was never completed. They are regarded as being the finest preserved fortifications of their time in Europe. These walls can still be walked, their length being about one and a half miles.

The many fine buildings include the **Berwick Barracks**, designed by Nicholas Hawksmoor (not Vanbrugh, as some people state) and built between 1717 and 1721. They were the first purpose-built barracks in Britain, and within them you'll find the **King's Own Scottish Borderers Museum**. This is another anomaly, as the KOSB, as the name suggests, is a Scottish regiment. Here visitors will learn about a regiment

Berwick-upon-Tweed Town Hall

UNION JACKS

3 Wallace Green, Berwick-upon-Tweed,
Northumberland TD15 1EB
Tel: 01289 306673
e-mail haddocksusan@hotmail.com

In the centre of Berwick, just off the main street, is the **Union Jacks** cafe and restaurant. Situated within a Georgian, stone built terrace dating back to the early 1700s, the restaurant has an attractive frontage adorned with two cut outs of men in traditional uniform either side of the door. Inside there is a neatly presented eating area with well spaced tables seating a total of 30 people. The staff are friendly and the service is efficient. The food is a classic range of simple, tasty dishes all freshly prepared to order and at reasonable prices. The restaurant has a table license which means that customers can enjoy a bottle of beer or a glass of wine with their meal. This establishment is popular with families as children are made very welcome.

The Union Jacks is owned and personally run by Susan Haddock and she is a busy woman who never seems to stop working. She has developed this into a well established, profitable business by maintaining high standards in all areas. She also develops the menus to keep them interesting and varied, making the most of seasonal produce wherever possible.

THE BROWN BEAR

Hide Hill, Berwick-upon-Tweed,
Northumberland TD15 1EQ
Tel: 01289 306214

In the centre of Berwick-upon-Tweed, you will find the characterful **Brown Bear Inn**. This town centre pub has been run by Susan Wakenshaw for the past four years and it is her delightful personality combined with lots of hard work that has made the establishment as popular as it is both for locals and visitors to the area. As soon as you enter you are aware of the wonderful atmosphere and you can expect outstanding service too. The building dates back to the 1860s and much of the historic character of the building has been retained both inside and out with the interior featuring high ceilings and the original bar.

Food is served each lunchtime from a simple menu offering tasty home cooked dishes that are served in good sized portions. The choices range from light snacks and more hearty dishes catering to all appetites. The Brown Bear attracts a broad range of customers, young and old, local and tourists, so you always can be sure of a warm reception. Live entertainment is provided for the enjoyment of all customers with live music each Friday night and the occasional disco. Open all day every day, the bar stocks a good selection of real ales from Vaux.

Royal Border Bridge, Berwick-upon-Tweed

Tweedmouth and Spittal. The oldest of these is the 17th-century **Berwick Bridge**, a handsome stone bridge with 15 arches completed in 1626. **The Royal Tweed Bridge** is the most modern, having been completed in 1928 with a concrete structure built to an iron bridge design. The enormous 126 feet high, 28 arch **Royal Border Bridge**, carrying the East Coast main-line railway, was built between 1847 and 1850 by Robert Stephenson.

The Berwick skyline is dominated by the imposing **Town Hall** with its clock tower and steeple, which rise to 150 feet, and which is often mistaken for a church. Built between 1754 and 1761, this fine building has a façade as elaborate as its well-documented history. On the ground floor, markets were held in the Exchange and shops and cells existed where now a gift shop and coffee house stand. Guided tours in the summer enable visitors to explore the upper storeys, where there are civic rooms and the former town gaol. A small **Cell Block Museum** is located there.

Facing Berwick Barracks is the church - one of the most interesting in the county. **Holy Trinity Church** was built between 1650 and 1652, during the Commonwealth of Oliver Cromwell, to replace a dilapidated medieval church which stood on the same site. It was built to one overall plan, and is one of the few Commonwealth churches in England.

that was raised in 1689 by the Earl of Leven, and which is still in existence today.

In the clock tower of the barracks is the **Berwick-upon-Tweed Borough Museum and Art Gallery**, which explores the history of the town. At nearby **Hutton Castle** lived Sir William Burrell, famous for collecting the works of art that can now be seen in the Burrell Art Gallery in Glasgow. But what is less well known is that he donated 300 works of art, sculpture and pottery to Berwick as well. This wonderful collection can be seen in the Borough Museum. Within the barracks is also the **Gymnasium Gallery**, opened in 1993 and housing changing exhibitions of contemporary art.

The Tweed estuary is spanned by three distinctive bridges linking the town centre with the communities of

MEADOW HILL GUEST HOUSE

Duns Road, Berwick-upon-Tweed,
Northumberland TD15 1UB
Tel: 01289 306325 Fax: 01289 306325
e-mail barryandhazel@meadow-hill.co.uk
website www.meadow-hill.co.uk

Just off the A1, heading towards Duns, travellers will easily find **Meadow Hill Guest House**. This is an area of Northumberland that has a great historic significance as the battle site of Halidon Hill, where in 1333 Edward III took Berwick from the Scots, is nearby. Meadow House itself is only 170 years old, originally having been built as a gentleman's residence, though more recent additions have been made to help make this a comfortable guest house. One of the most important developments was the provision of two ground floor suites that are suitable for disabled visitors and provided with every facility that could be required for an overnight stay. These rooms, together with their access to the rest of the guest house, has been recognised with an English Tourist Board Accessible Grading of level 2.

The rest of the house has also seen a complete refurbishment with the whole property always being maintained to the highest standards. There are a total of six bedrooms in all, with each being individually furnished and fully en-suite.

Breakfast, which is served in the guests' dining room, really will set you up for a busy day with plenty of choice ranging from fruit and cereals to cooked English breakfasts and kippers. Three course evening meals are also available by prior arrangement with the food being freshly prepared by the owner Hazel, who is a professionally trained cook. A selection of wine is also stocked and can be enjoyed with your meal if you wish.

THE MEADOW HOUSE BAR AND RESTAURANT

Great North Street,
Berwick-upon-Tweed,
Northumberland TD15 1UR
Tel: 01289 304173
website www.meadow/house.co.uk

Standing on the Great North Road at the northerly junction for Berwick-upon-Tweed is the magnificent **Meadow House**. This fine bar and restaurant has been run by Michael and Edith for over 20 years. Built at the beginning of the 19th century it was originally the Mayor's country house until it became a licensed premises in 1890 since when it has been supplying fine refreshments to passing trade. The original stone built house can be clearly distinguished from the later additions of a lounge bar and restaurant area. The result is a fine example of blending old and new, and those who venture inside will not be disappointed.

Beautifully decorated throughout, all the different areas are equally delightful with fine furnishings and attractive prints on the walls. This is very much a food oriented establishment with a wide ranging menu of fine cuisine catering to all tastes and appetites. The dishes on offer include fish, game, steak, pasta and much more, with all meals being freshly prepared and home cooked. To complement your meal there is a selection of wine from all over the world. The bar stocks a good range of drinks, with a selection of well-kept ales also on tap. Outside there is an attractive patio and garden area which can be enjoyed in warmer weather.

On the north west side of the town you will find all that remains of **Berwick Castle**. Built in the 13th century, it was demolished in 1850 to make way for the railway station, and the platform now occupies the site of the former Great Hall. The ruins are in the care of English Heritage.

AROUND BERWICK-UPON-TWEED

BAMBURGH
16 miles S of Berwick on the B1340

Bamburgh Castle is epic in scale, even by the standards of this coastline of spectacular castles, and dominates the village of the same name. Situated on a dramatic outcrop of the Whin Sill rock overlooking the sea, it was almost certainly the royal seat of the first kings of Bernicia from the 6th century onwards. The dynasty was founded by the Saxon King Ida in AD547 and mentioned in the "Anglo-Saxon Chronicle". Ida's grandson Ethelfrid united the kingdoms of Bernicia and Deira, and thus created Northumbria, a kingdom that stretched from the Humber to the Forth, and which in turn was ruled from Bamburgh.

In those days, the castle would have been of wood - a mighty stockade surrounding a great royal hall, sleeping quarters, stables, workshops and a garrison for troops. Later on, when Northumbria embraced Christianity, chapels would have been added, and the whole palace would have been an ostentatious declaration of the Northumbrian kings' power and wealth.

The present stone castle covers eight acres, and has a massive 12th century keep around which three baileys were

CANTY'S BRIG RIVERSIDE BAR AND RESTAURANT

Near Paxton, Berwick-upon-Tweed TD15 1SY
Tel: 01289 386255

Just a couple of miles from the A1, travellers will easily find **Canty's Brig Riverside Bar and Restaurant**, near to the village of Paxton. Built in 1846 of the local stone as a country pub serving the local farmers, the building has in recent years been refurbished and updated to provide a comfortable welcoming environment in which to enjoy a refreshing drink or a tasty meal. Surrounded by rolling fields, the pub is located next to the River Tweed and its extensive grounds incorporate a children's play area and outdoor seating running down to the river banks.

The present owner, who has only recently taken over, fell in love with the pub on his very first visit, and subsequently bought the premises! David Tobitt moved here from Islington in North London to bring his expertise to this already popular hostelry. As you enter the pub you will discover the cosy interior which has a rich red carpet throughout, stone faced walls and intimate little tables and chairs. In addition to the main bar with its open fire that is lit in winter, there are two restaurant areas. The Bistro and the Conservatory restaurant can be found downstairs and both have delightful views over the river. The menus offer an extensive selection catering to all tastes with the specialities being Wild Tweed Salmon and Border-reared steak. To enjoy with your meal there is an international wine list with an excellent New World selection.

HARBERTON GUEST HOUSE

181 Main Road, Spittal,
Berwick-upon-Tweed, Northumberland TD15 1RP
Tel: 01289 308813
e-mail: maurw@zetnet.co.uk   website www.harberton.com

Harberton Guest House can be found in the centre of Spittal at the southern end of the new Esplanade. This charming guest house is a Victorian Villa, having been built of the local stone in the late 1800s. The location is superb, with the pleasant garden giving direct access onto the promenade, and just yards from the water. This is the home of Rod and Maureen Watkins who have been running this as a guest house for over two years and are delighted to welcome guests old and new throughout the year. Much extended, the house can offer five guest bedrooms, two of which are en-suite, and all individually designed and

comfortably furnished. Guests can also make use of the large residents' lounge which has a beautiful view out over the sea front. Maureen is delighted to prepare evening meals on request and offers good, traditional home cooking. Vegetarians and special diets catered for. Hearty breakfasts are served from 8.00am and there is a fully licensed residents' bar. There is a secure car park and dogs are welcome by arrangement.

Spittal is just a couple of miles from Berwick-upon-Tweed and the A1 making this an ideal touring base or for an overnight stop en-route to Scotland.

THE COPPER KETTLE

21 Front Street, Bamburgh,
Northumberland NE69 7BW
Tel: 01668 214315
e-mail green@copperkettle.fastnet.co.uk

A visit to Bamburgh would not be complete without a visit to the **Copper Kettle Tea Rooms**. This is one of those very rare, traditional tea shops that England could once be proud of and that you can now rarely find in the modern day quest for fast food and trendy wine bars. Housed within a delightful, terraced, stone cottage, the building was inextricably linked with the fortunes of Bamburgh Castle from the day it was built in 1753 for the estate workers until 1956 when two sisters persuaded the castle trustees to sell it for conversion into a tea room. It has carried the name 'The Copper Kettle' from the day it opened and the kettle from which it takes its name is on display in the entrance hall.

The tea rooms have changed hands many times over the years with the present owners, Pat and Heather Green, having been in ownership since January 1999. They have carried out some extensive refurbishment and as a result many of the original features of the building can now be enjoyed at their best, including the stone mullioned windows and the richly carved oak panelling. Inside, visitors will find two delightful rooms, beautifully furnished and with seating for 40 people while the large patio garden can seat a further 20 in suitable weather. The menu offers an excellent range of cakes, snacks and light meals, all freshly prepared, home cooked and at very reasonable prices. The establishment is also licensed, so you can enjoy a refreshing bottle of beer or a glass of wine with your meal. The Copper Kettle Tea Rooms has established a far reaching reputation as one of the top tea rooms in England so it is certainly worth making it a priority on your list of places to visit.

Bamburgh Castle

Just offshore are the **Farne Islands**. This small group of 28 uninhabited islands of volcanic Whin Sill rock, just off the coast, provides a sanctuary for many species of sea birds, including kittiwake, fulmar, eider-duck, puffin, guillemot and tern. It is also home for a large colony of grey seal which can often be seen from the beach of the mainland.

constructed. The castle was extensively rebuilt and restored in the 18th and 19th centuries, latterly by the first Lord Armstrong.

Bamburgh is open to the public, and rooms on display include the Armoury, King's Hall, Court Room, Cross Hall, Bakehouse and Victorian Scullery, with collections of tapestries, ceramics, furniture and paintings. In the Laundry Room is an exhibition about the first Lord Armstrong and his many remarkable engineering inventions.

The village was the birthplace of Grace Darling, the celebrated Victorian heroine, who, in 1838, rowed out with her father from the **Longstone Lighthouse** in a ferocious storm to rescue the survivors of the steam ship "Forfarshire" which had foundered on the Farne Islands rocks. She died of tuberculosis only four years later, still only in her twenties, and is buried in the churchyard of St Aidan's. The **Grace Darling Museum**, in Radcliffe Road, also contains memorabilia of the famous rescue.

Puffin, Farne Islands

The islands have important Christian links, as it was on **Inner Farne** that St Cuthbert died in AD687. A little chapel was built here to his memory and restored in Victorian times. The nearby

Breeding Colonies, Farne Islands

THE VICTORIA HOTEL

Front Street, Bamburgh,
Northumberland NE69 7BP
Tel: 01668 214431 Fax: 01668 214404
e-mail enquiries@victoriahotel.net
website www.victoriahotel.net

Lying literally in the shadow of Bamburgh Castle, one of the most imposing buildings in the village of Bamburgh is **The Victoria Hotel**. Overlooking the village green, the attractive stone building dates back to the 1880s and retains many original features inside and out. The decorative detail has been carefully restored and sympathetically complemented by a stylish combination of traditional and modern decor with the overall feel being cosy and welcoming. When you first enter you will find the reception and bar area retaining the original polished wooden floors, while many of the downstairs reception rooms enjoy delightful views towards the Farne Islands.

The Victoria Hotel offers 29 comfortable bedrooms of varying sizes with every room having en-suite facilities and being provided with colour TV, telephone and complimentary hot drinks tray. A number of individually designed rooms have been created, using fine fabrics, furniture and antiques, and some have four poster beds. The stylish, airy Brasserie is open to all, and has been awarded an AA rosette for the standard of culinary flair with the kitchen presenting a wide range of innovative dishes prepared using the freshest of local produce and featuring a number of local specialities. Other facilities here at The Victoria include an indoor children's play area, function room and traditional musical entertainment in the summer months.

MARKET CROSS GUEST HOUSE

1 Church Street, Belford,
Northumberland NE70 7LS
Tel: 01668 213013
e-mail: details@marketcross.net
website: www.marketcross.net

Situated on the main street of Belford, just one mile from the A1 and 15 miles from the Scottish border, is the charming **Market Cross Guest House**. Part of a stone built terrace, the house dates back to the 18th century and is a listed building. The well-presented frontage features a neatly painted green door with hanging wall baskets on each side and every window having a colourful window box. The guest house has been run by Jill and John Hodge for three years coming here from previous careers as a teacher and policeman respectively. In the relatively short time they have been here, the Market Cross has become very well established and developed a

fine reputation for a friendly welcome and comfortable accommodation. The Hodges can offer four bedrooms in all, each with en-suite facilities, colour TV and tea and coffee making tray. Each room has been individually designed and tastefully furnished and are very homely and well cared for. Guests here can also make use of the superb courtyard and gardens, at the rear of the property, in summer months. Evening meals are not provided but there are a number of lovely pubs within the town that do serve food. This would make an ideal base for touring the stunning Northumbrian coastline, castles and countryside. English Tourist Board Highly Commended and AA 4à graded. No smoking.

Lighthouse, Farne Islands

whose broad main street contains some interesting old shops and a fine old coaching inn, reflecting the fact that this was once an important town on the Great North Road. Today it is an ideal holiday base, standing on the edge of the **Kyloe Hills**, where there are some worthwhile walks, and close to the long golden beaches and rocky outcrops of the coast.

Tower House was built in medieval times by Prior Castell, according to legend, on the site of Cuthbert's cell. Landings are permitted on **Inner Farne** and **Staple Island**, though times are restricted for conservation reasons and advance booking is urged in the busy times of year.

BELFORD
14 miles S of Berwick off the A1

Belford is an attractive village of stone houses

Cheviot Hills, Belford

Kyloe Hills, Belford

St Cuthbert's Cave, on the moors one mile east of the A1 and to the north of the town, is only accessible by foot. It is completely natural, and concealed by a great overhanging rock surrounded by woodland. It is believed that the saint's body lay here on its much interrupted journey across Northumbria. From the summit of nearby **Greensheen Hill** there are superb views of the coast and of the Cheviots to the west.

WELL HOUSE COFFEE SHOP

33 High Street, Belford,
Northumberland NE70 7NG
Tel: 01668 213779
e-mail: wellhousecoffeeshop@hotmail.com

On the main road running through the centre of
Belford you will find the cosy and welcoming **Well
House Coffee Shop**. Dating back to the 17th century
it is not surprising to learn that the site was once
used for a coaching inn, of which there were many
at one time along the Great North Road. The four
hundred year old building is well preserved and has recently been refurbished and renovated by the
owners David and Lilian Eddy. The interior retains its characterful ambiance and is tastefully and
elegantly furnished in a traditional style. Primarily a coffee shop, the Well House is open from 10am
serving a selection of coffee and teas, light meals and refreshments with various cakes and other sweet
things. The food is freshly prepared to order, much is home made and everyone is sure to find something

to suit their taste, like a delicious home baked cheese or fruit
scone, or a traditional 'singin hinny' served hot from the
griddle. The coffee shop is closed Mondays, except bank
holidays, and Tuesdays from November to February.

In addition to the coffee shop David and Lilian also offer
a self-contained apartment for short breaks and week long
holiday rental. This accommodation, recently converted from
a former hay-loft, is furnished to an exceptionally high
standard, and is worthy of 5 Star grading. Ring for brochure
and details of rates and availability.

THE RED LION

Main Road, Milfield, Northumberland NE71 6JD
Tel: 01668 216224 Fax: 01668 216224

The Red Lion is the only pub in the small village of Milfield, and it is
thought to be one of the oldest in Northumberland. Built around 1740 the
large stone structure features some delightful Venetian windows and is a
listed building. Originally this was a drovers inn and here the drover and
their flocks would have found shelter and hospitality on their long journey
to market.

Today, the Red Lion welcomes a loyal local following together with a
large number of visitors to the area. The imposing building is hard to miss
and enjoys a prime position on the A697 between Wooler and Coldstream.
Inside you will find a large open lounge bar and public bar with both being comfortably furnished
and kept warm with a large open fire in winter. Behind the bar they stock a good range of beer and

lager, with some of the selection of real ales coming from
the Black Sheep brewery. Food is served each lunch time
and evening from a menu offering a selection of dishes,
all freshly prepared and home cooked. The kitchen is
supervised by Heather Logan, while her husband John
looks after the bar. The couple have only been here 12
months and have spent a lot of time and effort in
refurbishing the property to update and improve the
facilities. In addition to the pub they can also offer bed
and breakfast and self catering accommodation. There
are two family sized rooms for overnight stays, provided
with either a full en-suite bath or shower room. Ring for
details of the self-catering holiday home.

DUDDO
7 miles SW of Berwick on the B6354

Close to the village are the **Duddo Stones**, one of Northumberland's most important ancient monuments. This ancient stone circle, which now consists of five upright stones over seven feet high, dates back to around 2000 BC, and can only be reached from the village by foot.

FORD & ETAL
13 miles SW of Berwick off the B6354

Ford and Etal are twin estate villages built in the late 19th century. Etal, on the B6354, is an attractive village,

Etal Church

within which are the ruins of the 14th century castle, destroyed in 1497 by King James IV of Scotland on his way to Flodden, and now in the care of English Heritage and open to the public. The **Church of the Blessed Virgin Mary** was built in 1858 by Lady Augusta Fitz-Clarence in memory of her husband and daughter.

The twin village of Ford is a "model" village with many beautiful stone buildings and well-tended gardens. Dating originally from the 14th century, but heavily restored in the 19th century, Ford Castle was the home of Louisa Ann, Marchioness of Waterford. In 1860 she built the village school and from 1862 until 1883 spent her time decorating it with murals depicting biblical scenes. As models she used local families and their children. Now known as Lady Waterford Hall, it is open to the public.

At **Heatherslaw**, between the two villages, is the **Heatherslaw Railway**, a

15 inch gauge railway that runs to Etal Castle, and close by is **Heatherslaw Corn Mill**, a working 18th century watermill which is open to the public. About two and a half miles south west is the small village of Milfield, where there is a 16th century tower house called **Coupland Castle**.

HORNCLIFFE
4 miles W of Berwick off the A698

About five miles upstream of Berwick the village of Horncliffe can be reached by just one road that leads into and out of the village, making it feel rather remote. Many visitors are unaware of the existence of the river, but there is nothing more pleasant than wandering down one of the paths leading to the banks to watch the salmon fishermen on a summer's evening.

Not far from the village the River Tweed is spanned by the **Union Suspension Bridge** linking Scotland and

THE FISHERS ARMS

Main Street, Horncliffe, Nr. Berwick-upon-Tweed, Northumberland TD15 2XW
Tel: 01289 386022

The Fishers Arms stands on the main street in the fine village of Horncliffe and has recently been taken over by husband and wife team, Amanda and Adrian. This attractive inn dates back nearly 200

years and inevitably has had many links with the local fishing community. Inside you will find a warm welcome and plenty of atmosphere with many original features including exposed stone walls, covered in old pictures, and open fires. There is a good sized bar and lounge area, furnished with traditional wooden tables and chairs. Open Monday to Friday lunchtime and evenings and all day Saturday and Sunday, the Fishers Arms boasts a comprehensive food menu plus a good selection of daily specials, all home-cooked and freshly prepared. The dishes range from light bar snacks to good, hearty lunches, with all tastes catered for.

If you would like to stay at this friendly establishment for a little longer, then you will find two comfortable letting rooms available for overnight stays - ideal if you have partaken of a little too much of the pub's excellent Real Ales. Amanda and Adrian have plans to refurbish and update the property, while making every effort to retain the original character, so there could be some new developments by the time you visit.

England, built in 1820 by Sir Samuel Browne, who also invented the wrought-iron chain links used in its construction. Telford studied the bridge when designing the Menai Bridge in Wales, and used Browne's chain links when building it. The graceful structure, 480 feet long, was Britain's first major suspension bridge to carry vehicular traffic, and although not carrying a major road, it is still possible to drive over it.

LINDISFARNE, OR HOLY ISLAND
10 miles S of Berwick off the A1

Northumberland's northern coastline is dominated by one outstanding feature - Lindisfarne, also known as Holy Island.

Visitors can get across only at low tide along the three-mile long causeway from Beal. Tide tables are published locally and are displayed at each end of the road and there are refuges part way along for those who fail to time it correctly. Alternatively there are bus services from Berwick, which run

Lindisfarne from Ross Back Sands

Lindisfarne Priory

their precious gospels with them. These have, miraculously, survived and are now in the safety of the British Museum. Facsimiles are kept on Lindisfarne and can be seen in the 12th-century parish church on the island.

St Cuthbert also came here, living on a tiny islet as a hermit before seeking even further seclusion on the Farne Islands. A cross marks the site of his tiny chapel.

according to tides. As you cross, note the 11th-century **Pilgrims' Way**, marked by stakes, still visible about 200 metres south of the modern causeway. This route was in use until comparatively recent times.

This, most evocative of English islands, was known as Lindisfarne until the 11th century when a group of Benedictine monks settled here giving it the name Holy Island, although both names are now used. The ruins of their great sandstone **Lindisfarne Priory**, in massive Romanesque style with great pillars, can still be explored. They are now looked after by English Heritage

The links with early Christianity go further back than the Benedictines. It was here, in AD635, that St Aidan and his small community of Irish monks came from Iona to found a base from which to convert northern England to Christianity. This led to the island being called one of the cradles of English Christianity.

These early monks are also remembered for producing some of the finest surviving examples of Celtic art - the richly decorated **Lindisfarne Gospels**, dating from the 7th century. When the island was invaded by Vikings in the 9th century the monks fled taking

Lindisfarne is the finishing point for the 62-mile long **St. Cuthbert's Way**, a long distance footpath which opened in 1996. It finishes at Melrose, across the Scottish border, and along the way passes through the Northumberland

St Aidens Statue, Lindisfarne

THE WHITE SWAN

51 Main Street, Lowick, Berwick-upon-Tweed, Northumberland TD15 2UD
Tel: 01289 388249

On the main road in the centre of Lowick is the well-established **White Swan** inn. This traditional country hostelry has been under the ownership of Roy and Brenda Cossar for 32 years, and it is not surprising to learn that this has become a popular, successful pub. Roy and Brenda are very hands on and can always be found serving the customers from behind the bar with a friendly smile, working in the kitchen or in the restaurant.

The fine building dates back to the 17th century and has a well documented history. The exterior is simple and uncluttered with car parking provided across the front of the building and to the side. The interior comprises a public and lounge bar, 35-cover restaurant and a games room with pool table

and juke box. Each of the areas are cosy and comfortable and any would be suitable for simply enjoying a refreshing drink from the well-stocked bar. Food is offered from a varied, well-balanced menu with plenty of choice to suit even the most discerning. All meals are home cooked and use fresh local produce wherever possible. The house specialities are the scotch broth and steak and kidney pie, so these come heartily recommended. This establishment is clearly well loved and every customer can be assured of a warm and friendly welcome.

VICTORIA HOTEL

3 Castle Street, Norham,
Northumberland TD15 2LQ
Tel: 01289 382437

In the small village of Norham, lying in the shadow of the castle, is a traditional village inn, **The Victoria Hotel**. Enjoying a picturesque setting in the delightful village, the inn dates back to the early 19th century and has a distinctive Victorian air. The unassuming exterior conceals a clean, bright and welcoming interior. There is a well presented lounge bar and public bar which have been attractively furnished to maintain a cosy and comfortable feel. Behind the bar you will find a good range of beer and lager with a varying selection of real ales

kept on tap, including John Smiths. Food is served each lunch time with a traditional range of bar meals and snacks. All dishes are freshly prepared and home cooked.

If you are looking for somewhere to stay while exploring this area, or en-route to Scotland, then The Victoria Hotel can offer two rooms for bed and breakfast. The comfortable rooms share a bathroom, and are provided with a TV and complimentary tea and coffee making facilities. The inn is run by Neil and Maureen Turnbull who have been here for nearly three years and have contributed greatly to its current popularity. They have plenty of plans and ideas for gradually updating and improving the facilities, so watch this space!

Lindisfarne Priory

LOWICK
8 miles S of Berwick on the B6353

Lowick is a quiet farming community which contains only a few shops and a couple of pubs. About a mile east of the village are the earthworks of a former castle. The Norman church was replaced by the present **St John the Baptist Church.**

NORHAM
6 miles SW of Berwick on the B6470

Norham is a neat, historical village that sits on the banks of the Tweed, and up until 1836 was an enclave of the County Palatinate of Durham surrounded by Northumberland on the south, east and west, and Scotland on the north. **Norham Castle** was built in the 12th century by a bishop of Durham and stands on a site of great natural strength guarding a natural ford over the river. It withstood repeated attacks in the 13th and 14th centuries and was thought to be impregnable. However, in 1513 it was stormed by the forces of James IV on his way to Flodden and partially destroyed.

Although it was later rebuilt, the castle was again destroyed by the Scots in 1530, and had lost its importance as a defensive stronghold by the end of the 16th century. The castle is now under the care of English Heritage, and is open to the public all year.

Norham's privately-owned **Station Museum** is located on the former Tweedmouth-Kelso branch line. The museum features the original signal box, booking office, porter's room model railway.

Each year in Norham an unusual ceremony still takes place which has long Christian associations. **The**

National Park and the Cheviot Hills. On the English side, it is managed by both Northumberland County Council and the Northumberland National Park. It's clearly marked along its whole length, and trail guides and leaflets are available.

Lindisfarne Castle was established in Tudor times as yet another fortification to protect the exposed flank of Northumbria from invasion by the Scots. In 1902 it was bought by Edward Hudson, the owner of "Country Life", and he employed the great Edwardian architect Sir Edward Lutyens to rebuild and restore it as a private house. It is now in the care of the National Trust, and the house and its small walled garden are open to the public during the summer months.

Holy Island village is a community of around 170 people who work in farming, in the island's distillery (noted for excellent traditional mead) and in the tourist trade. Much of the island is also a nature reserve, with wildflowers and a wide variety of seabirds. **St Mary's Church** in the village has some fine Saxon stonework above the chancel arch.

FAIRHOLM

East Ord, Berwick-upon-Tweed, Northumberland TD15 2NS
Tel: 01289 305370

You will find **Fairholm Bed and Breakfast** just a short distance from the centre of Berwick, in East Ord. This delightful, stone built bungalow is the home of Beth Welsh and has been for over 30 years. There are just two guest bedrooms and Beth provides a warm, Northumbrian welcome to all her residents, many of whom will have stayed here before. What better recommendation could there be? This is a real home from home, with the whole house being kept meticulously clean and tidy and in

good decorative order. The comfortable rooms are individually decorated and finished with those little touches that show that the place is well loved.

There is a double bedroom which has an en-suite bathroom, while the other room is a twin and has the use of a bathroom just down the hallway. Each morning Beth provides a choice of cooked breakfast and an evening meal can be provided by prior arrangement. This 150 year old bungalow enjoys an elevated site in this tranquil village and would make an ideal touring base and being so close to the A1 would be a perfect overnight stop en-route to or from Scotland. Fairholm has an English Tourist Board Four Star grading.

THE SALMON INN

East Ord, Berwick-upon-Tweed, Northumberland TD15 2NS
Tel: 01289 305227

A little way out from the centre of Berwick, still within the loop of the A1, is the area called East Ord. Here is the **Salmon Inn**, an ideal stopping place if you are travelling through the area, as it is so close to the A1. This is a friendly and lively establishment, popular with locals as well as tourists. Here you will find a good range of beer and lager, as well as the usual selection of wine, spirits and soft drinks, and a choice of three real ales which are regularly rotated.

Food is served each lunch time from a modest menu of traditional meals and snacks with the fresh, wholesome dishes offering good value for money. There is a public bar and lounge areas which have recently been refurbished and updated with new furniture and a lovely thick carpet. This is all a result of the hard work put in by the relatively new husband and wife team that now manage the Salmon Inn, Douglas and Mary Hope.

They have also renovated the outside of this 1840s building by cleaning up the stone work and repainting the windows and doors. They haven't finished all the work yet however, with future plans including the addition of a conservatory dining area.

Blessing of the Nets is held at midnight on 13th February to mark the beginning of the salmon fishing season. The service is held by lantern light, with the clergyman standing in a boat in the middle of the river.

TILLMOUTH

9 miles SW of Berwick on the A698

The village of Tillmouth lies along the banks of the River Till, a tributary of the Tweed, which is crossed by the 15th-century **Twizel Bridge** although a more modern structure now carries the A698 over the river. Up until the building of the 1727 Causey Arch in County Durham, the old Twizel Bridge, with a span of 90 feet, had the largest span of any bridge in Britain. There are some lovely walks here and a well-signed footpath leads to the ruins of **Twizel Castle**, and, on the opposite bank, the remains of **St Cuthbert's Chapel**, dating from the 18th or 19th centuries, but incorporating some medieval stonework.

Twizel Bridge

TWEEDMOUTH

1 mile S of Berwick off the A1

Tweedmouth and Spittal, on the "English" side of the Tweed estuary, are mainly suburbs of Berwick. In mid-July a ceremony is held in Tweedmouth which dates back to 1292 and celebrates the fact that the River Tweed, one of the best salmon rivers in Britain, reaches the sea here. The local schools hold a ballot to elect a "Salmon Queen" and her crowning marks the beginning of Feast week which centres around a church service but also involves lots of festivities and a traditional salmon supper.

WAREN MILL

15 miles SE of Berwick on the B1342

Waren Mill is a small village situated on **Budle Bay**, a large inlet of flats and sand where vast numbers of wading birds and wildfowl come to feed. Caution should be taken when walking on the flats, as sections quickly become cut off at high tide.

ALNWICK

Alnwick (pronounced "Annick") is one of the most impressive towns in Northumberland. It still has the feel and appearance of a great medieval military and commercial centre, being an important market town since the granting of its charter in 1291. It is dominated by the massive bulk of **Alnwick Castle**, which began, like most of the Northumberland castles, as a Norman motte and bailey. In the 12th century this was replaced by a stone castle, which was much added to over the centuries. In 1309 it came into the possession of Henry de Percy, who strengthened the fortifications. Henry's great grandson was made an earl, and

THE GEORGIAN GUEST HOUSE

3/5 Hotspur Street, Alnwick, Northumberland NE66 1QE
Tel: 01665 602398 Fax: 01665 602398
e-mail georgianhouse@eggconnect.net

The Georgian Guest House is in the centre of Alnwick within easy reach of the many attractions of this delightful town including the pedestrian entrance to the new Alnwick Gardens (opening October 2001). Built in the mid-1800s the house has a traditional, creamy stone frontage. The front is decorated with a colourful display of hanging baskets, in season, while to the rear there is a small private garden.

Access for off-street parking is through an archway to the side of the main building.

This charming, two diamond guest house offers four, en-suite guest rooms, all comfortably furnished and neatly presented. The house has a very homely atmosphere and a friendly welcome with personal service is offered by the owner, Peter Gibb. Guests can enjoy a freshly cooked, full English breakfast in the morning served in the private guests' dining room. Evening meals are not available, however there are a number of excellent pubs and restaurants nearby.

The location of the guest house makes this a popular choice for those wanting a central base for exploring the Northumberland coast.

GRANNIES

18 Narrowgate, Alnwick, Northumberland
Tel: 01665 602394

The small cosy establishment of **Grannies** is something of a local institution, and well known to anyone who has visited Alnwick. What appears to be simply a small delicatessen is much, much more.

The ground floor does in fact offer a delicatessen which stocks an excellent range of cheeses and hams, including a number of local cheeses and air dried ham produced at nearby Bamburgh. The sandwich takeaway provides a choice of freshly prepared sandwiches and rolls catering to all tastes, with traditional as well as more innovative fillings, with a tasty selection of homemade savouries and cakes.

If you investigate further, you will find that downstairs there is a cosy tea room, popular with locals, shoppers and tourists. The decor is reminiscent of a Victorian kitchen and the beams and walls are decorated with memorabilia consistent with the theme. Here you will find a wide ranging menu offering dishes to suit all tastes and appetites. Locally sourced produce, including the cheeses and hams mentioned above and fresh local salmon, are used wherever possible, and the home made cakes are positively irresistible. To enjoy with your meal, or simply on its own, we can recommend the freshly ground coffees.

Grannies is housed within a stone built terrace not far from the popular castle and has a neatly painted blue and gold exterior decorated with flowering baskets in summer months. Nearby is the infamous 'dirty bottles' pub where the publican stacked empty bottles in the window of the pub. The publican later died of a heart attack and local legend has is that anyone who touches the bottles will also die. As a result, the bottles have remained virtually untouched for over 100 years.

Alnwick Castle

was commissioned to make improvements. However, these were largely swept away in the 1850s and 1860s when the 4th Duke commissioned the Victorian architect Anthony Salvin to transform the castle into a great country house with all modern comforts while recapturing its former medieval glory. The castle is still the home of the Percys to this day, and is a favourite location for making films, including the Harry Potter film, where it doubles as Hogwart's School.

eleven earls later, the male Percy line died out. It then passed through the female line to Sir Hugh Smithson, who took the Percy name and was created Duke of Northumberland.

In the 18th century, the castle was falling into disrepair, and Robert Adam

A number of rooms are open to the public, and amongst its treasures are paintings by Titian, Tintoretto, Canaletto and Van Dyck, collections of Meissen china and superb furniture.

THE ODDFELLOWS ARMS

Narrowgate, Alnwick,
Northumberland NE66 1JN
Tel: 01665 605363

Lying in the shadow of Alnwick Castle, in the centre of the town, is the long established **Oddfellows Arms**. Dating back to the mid-1700s the pub lies in a street of large stone building which now house bed and breakfasts, restaurants and antique shops. This really is a delightful town to explore with the ancient narrow streets containing a variety of quaint little shops in which to while away an afternoon.

The Oddfellows Arms is well placed to offer refreshment during a day's exploring or shopping and welcomes a number of visitors as well as being popular with the locals. The cosy interior features a lounge and a public bar and there are plenty of alcoves and corners in which to tuck yourself away for a quiet drink. The bar stocks the leading brands of beer and lager so you are sure to find something to suit. Food is served each lunch time and evening offering a selection of snacks and meals. The menu is regularly updated to make the most of local and seasonal produce and there are some excellent value specials. If you would like a place to stay in the centre of town then you need look no further, as there are three rooms available for bed and breakfast. Each has a washbasin, TV and tea and coffee making facilities, and there is a shared bathroom.

ROSEWORTH

Alnwick, Northumberland NE66 2PR
Tel: 01665 603911
e-mail roseworthann@freeserve.co.uk

Roseworth is an absolutely delightful bed and breakfast, owned and personally run by Anne Bowden. Ann has been running this business for over 12 years, and it is not surprising to learn that the guest house is often busy! Her charming home may only have built in 1947 but it has established itself well, presenting a front that is covered with climbers most of the year round and a mass of green ivy. There is a profusion of tubs, flower beds and hanging baskets too which add colour through the seasons.

The garden is a true delight having been well designed and landscaped to offer elegant flower beds around a pristine lawn and with a large pond in which fish swim and irises thrive.

Inside, the house has the air of a well loved and cared for home. Ann keeps everything neat and clean while making all her guests feel right at home. There are three bedrooms in all, each with an en-suite or private bathroom, and all have a TV and tea and coffee making facilities. The home cooked breakfasts are a great way to start a day's sight-seeing, or walking, and evening meals can be provided by arrangement. Open all year.

THE BEACHES RESTAURANT AND B&B

Northumberland Street, Alnmouth,
Northumberland NE66 2RJ
Tel: 01665 830443 Fax: 01665 830443
e-mail le.chef@breathemail.net

On Northumberland Street, in the heart of the small town of Alnmouth, you will find **The Beaches Restaurant and Bed and Breakfast**. This cosy establishment has been run by Donald and Susan Hall for 18 years and they have developed a far reaching reputation for serving quality food and providing comfortable accommodation. The small building from which the businesses are run dates back to 1725 when it was originally built as a granary. It later became a Methodist Church and it wasn't until the late 20th century that it was converted for its present use.

The Beaches Restaurant is a charming and characterful room, decorated with a sea faring theme. The atmosphere is cosy and intimate, enhanced by the low ceilings and subdued lighting, making this a ideal venue for a romantic dinner, though equally popular for quick lunches. The menu offers a wide range of innovative choices, with the creative selection continually being updated. It is not only fish and seafood that feature, though you can be assured that this will always be of the freshly and highest quality, you will also find steak, game and vegetarian dishes to choose from. If you would like an alcoholic drink with your meal, visitors are invited to bring their own wine. In addition to the restaurant is the bed and breakfast accommodation with two, double en-suite guest rooms available. The rooms are homely, comfortable and provided with a TV and tea and coffee tray. There is also a self-catering unit, quaintly called 'The Beach Hut', which can sleep up to six people.

Alnwick Market

overlooks the River Aln, and dates from the 15th century. It was unusual in a place as lawless as Northumberland at that time to build a church as large and as splendid as St Michael's.

The popular and colourful **Alnwick Fair**, dating from the 13th century, takes place each June.

There is also an extremely important archaeological museum and extensive archive collections, as well as the **Royal Northumberland Fusiliers Museum** in The Abbot's Tower.

Hulne Park, landscaped by the great (and Northumbrian-born) **Capability Brown**, encompasses the ruins of **Hulne Priory**, the earliest Carmelite foundation in England, dating from 1242.

Alnwick town itself is worthy of an afternoon's exploration with its ancient narrow streets retaining such evocative names as Fenkle Street, Pottergate, Green Batt, Bondgate Without and Bondgate Within. One road leads through the narrow arch of **Hotspur Tower**, the one surviving part of the town's fortifications, built by the second Duke of Northumberland in the 15th century. And all that's left of the once mighty **Alnwick Abbey** is its 15th century gatehouse, situated just beyond Canongate Bridge.

St Michael's Church

AROUND ALNWICK

ALNMOUTH
3 miles E of Alnwick off the A1068

Alnmouth is a small resort with fine sands and a golf course, clearly visible from the express trains of the East Coast main line that pass by. The village dates back to the 8th century and was established as a planned port in the Middle Ages. John Paul Jones, the Scot who founded the American navy, bombarded the port during the American War of Independence.

It is the starting point of many excellent walks along superb stretches

Alnmouth Sands

THE COACH INN

Main Street, Lesbury, Alnwick,
Northumberland NE66 3PP
Tel: 01665 830865

Lesbury can be found just off the A1068, not far from Alnmouth and here in the centre of the village on the main street you will find the historic **Coach Inn**. Dating back to the 1700s the frontage is a delight, with the original stonework having been cleaned and restored. Also to the front is a patio area where there are a number of picnic tables at which to enjoy a drink in warm weather.

The interior features low, beamed ceilings and traditional, wooden furnishings - just as a real country pub should be. The atmosphere is cosy and comfortable with the landlords, Chris and Margaret Bignell, extending a friendly welcome to all who pass through the doors. The location, not far from the dramatic Northumberland coastline, makes this a popular haunt not only for locals but also tourists. Many come to sample the delicious home cooked food which is offered from a wide ranging menu each lunch time and evening in the separate restaurant. The dishes are freshly prepared to order and utilise local produce wherever possible. The imaginative menu would certainly appeal to all who appreciate good cooking. If you prefer a lively night out then a regular pub quiz is held each Wednesday - to be participated in or avoided as you prefer!

DOXFORD FARM COTTAGES

Chathill, Nr. Alnwick, Northumberland NE67 5DY
Tel: 01665 579348 Fax: 01665 579331
website www.cottageguide.co.uk/doxfordfarmcottages

Doxford Farm is a working farm situated in 600 acres of unspoilt wooded countryside, four miles from the sea and midway between Alnwick and Belford. Here, self-catering accommodation is available in one of seven stone-built cottages or a converted farmhouse annex. All the cottages have been carefully, and tastefully, restored and modernised to provide comfortable accommodation and all are well equipped to ensure a relaxing holiday. The smallest of the cottages sleeps just two while the largest sleep seven in three bedrooms. Cots and high chairs can be provided if there are young children in the party and dogs are welcome for a small additional charge. There are five miles of wooded and lakeside walks and trails within the farm boundaries and it is a safe distance to the

main road, so children can play safely. Leaflets can be provided to help you enjoy your walks to the full. The lake and small pond hold brown trout and guests are welcome to fish free of charge.

In addition with providing you with somewhere to stay, Sarah and Tom Shell also run Doxford Country Store and Coffee Shop. The store sells a huge variety of gift ware, carefully selected from around the world, with cotton throws, rustic baskets, recycled glass, country American paints, wooden boxes and much, much more. The Country Clothing shop stocks an exclusive range of Danish clothing, denim from Ireland, handbags from Italy and a large selection of Cashmere knitwear and sweatshirts. The coffee shop is well known for its home-made cakes and scones, also serving a delicious selection of sandwiches and soups, and is an ideal place for a refreshing snack after enjoying one of the local walks. Meals can be enjoyed inside or out in the beautiful courtyard.

of coastline either southwards, past extensive dunes to Warkworth, or north to the former fishing village of Boulmer.

AMBLE
7 miles SE of Alnwick on the A1068

Amble is a small port on the mouth of the River Coquet, once important for the export of coal, but now enjoying new prosperity as a marina and sea-fishing centre, with a carefully restored harbour.

A mile offshore lies 14 acre **Coquet Island** which had a monastic foundation known as Cocwadae in Anglo Saxon times, and a Benedictine cell dating from the 14th century. The ruins of the cell have been incorporated into the island's lighthouse. Coquet Island had a reputation in former times for causing shipwrecks but is now a celebrated bird sanctuary, noted for colonies of terns, puffins and eider

River Coquet, Amble

ducks. Managed by the Royal Society for the Protection of Birds, the island can be visited by boat from Amble on pre-arranged trips.

BEADNELL
10 miles NE of Alnwick on the B1340

Beadnell is a small fishing village with a harbour and some important 18th-century lime kilns that are now owned by the National Trust. Running eastwards from the harbour into the sea is **Ebb's Nook**, a narrow strip of land with the scant remains of 13th century **St Ebba's Chapel**, dedicated to the sister of King Oswald, King of Northumbria. This is a delightful stretch of coast, and keen walkers can follow the coastline either by shore path or along the B1340 past **St Aidan's Dunes** (owned by the National Trust) to Seahouses.

CHATHILL
8 miles N of Alnwick off the A1

Close to Chathill is **Preston Tower**, built by Sir Robert Harbottle, Sheriff of Northumberland, in 1392. The walls are seven feet thick, and inside are fine tunnel-vaulted rooms which have changed little over the centuries. Two turret rooms have been simply furnished in the style of the period and there are also displays of historic and local information. Preston Tower is open all year round during daylight hours.

CHILLINGHAM
11 miles NW of Alnwick off the B6348

Chillingham is a pleasant estate village best known for the herd of wild, horned white cattle that roam parkland close to **Chillingham Castle**. They are perhaps the purest surviving specimens of the wild cattle that once roamed the hills and forests of Britain (see panel on page 115).

THE PACK HORSE INN

Ellingham, Chathill, Northumberland NE67 5HA
Tel: 01665 589292

Less than a mile from the A1, about 8 miles north of Alnwick, **The Pack Horse Inn** can be located at one end of the picturesque main street of the village of Ellingham. The Inn has graced the village for over 150 years and provides a congenial meeting place for villagers and visitors alike. Once part of the famous Haggerston Castle Estate it was used in the mid-19th century as a counting house where the farm workers would be paid, and then usually went through to the bar to spend it all!

The bar area is cosy and comfortable, with the traditional style and character of this building not having been lost over the years. Well kept real ales are served here, enjoyed by a number of local characters, as well as by the many visitors to the area. There is a cosy restaurant offering a varied menu in intimate surroundings, the perfect place in which to sample and enjoy the Inn's excellent home-cooking. If you are looking for something a little less formal a selection of bar meals are also

available, which can be enjoyed in the pretty beer garden at the rear of the pub. The garden offers beautiful views over miles of surrounding countryside and proves to be a real sun trap in the warm summer months.

The present owners, Maureen and Diane, provide their guests with superb bed and breakfast accommodation in five bedrooms, all having full en-suite facilities and fully equipped to cater for your every need. There is also a self-catering holiday cottage available for short breaks and weekly lets.

PROCTOR'S STEAD COTTAGES

Proctor's Stead, Craster, Alnwick,
Northumberland NE66 3TF
Tel: 01665 576613

Dating from the 1800s the stone cottages at **Proctor's Stead** have been created from former outbuildings by Robert and Ruth Davidson. Comprising part of their own farm, the semi-retired couple have put a lot of care and effort into the sensitive conversion of the existing buildings to create two delightful holiday homes. Both are comfortably furnished and tastefully decorated, and come provided with all the essentials for a relaxing holiday away from home. The basic layout is the same for both cottages, each having a large kitchen/dining room which affords fine views to the front and rear of the properties.

The kitchens are fully equipped with electric cooker, washing machine, tumble dryer, microwave and fridge and all bed linen is provided at no extra cost so the only thing a guest needs to bring is towels. Dunstanburgh View offers one double and one twin room while Seascape is slightly larger with two double rooms and a twin. There is a cot and high chair available and ample car parking is provided. There are many activities and places to visit within a short drive of Proctor's Stead, with the coastline alone having much to offer. This would be an ideal base for a week long break and is readily accessible from the main A1.

Preston Tower, Chathill

Chillingham Castle is beautifully sited within a 365-acre park, but sadly fell into ruin in the 1930s. It has now been restored, revealing a medieval fortress complete with jousting course,

dungeon and torture chamber. The castle and surrounding gardens are open to the public from May to September. Two signposted walks have been laid out through Chillingham Woods, giving superb views over the surrounding countryside.

Just outside the village is the National Trust-owned hill fort called **Ross Castle**, once a vital beacon site visible as far afield as the Scottish hills and Holy Island. The whole area was thrown into chaos in 1804 when an over-enthusiastic warden lit the beacon by mistake.

CRASTER
6 miles NE of Alnwick off the B1339

Craster is a small, unpretentious fishing village which is nationally known for its oak-smoked kippers. At one time herring were caught around this coast in vast quantities, but a possible combination of over-fishing and pollution resulted in a decline in numbers, so the fish now have to be imported. During the kipper curing season visitors can peer into the smoking sheds where the herring are hung over smouldering piles of oak chips.

South of Craster is **Howick Hall**, built in 1782, and having long associations

CHILLINGHAM WILD CATTLE PARK

Chillingham, Alnwick, Northumberland NE66 5NP
Tel & Fax: 01668 215250

In the 365 acres of the **Chillingham Wild Cattle Park** you'll find the only herd of wild white cattle in Britain. These magnificent animals are descended from the cattle that once roamed Britain's forests long ago, and are truly wild. No outside blood has been introduced into a herd whose population can vary from 40 to 60. They can be potentially dangerous, so you should be accompanied by an experienced warden at all times when viewing them! The park is also home to a wide variety of wildlife, from red

squirrels to fallow deer. Opening times: Beginning of April to end of October each year, from 10.00-12.00 and 14.00-17.00, Monday, Wednesday, Thursday, Friday & Saturday; 14-17.00 on Sunday; closed all day Tuesday. Admission charge

THE JOLLY FISHERMAN

Craster, Northumberland NE66 3TR
Tel: 01665 576461 Fax: 01665 576461
website www.come.to/the jollyfisherman.com

Enjoying probably the best site in the whole of Craster, the **Jolly Fisherman** public house is a great place to stop for a refreshing drink or meal while exploring the area. Stunning views can be enjoyed both from the beer garden and the elevated lounge with both looking out over the picturesque harbour, sea wall and the sea beyond. In addition to the large lounge there is also a small bar area and both are comfortable and relaxing.

The pub has a happy atmosphere, due in no small part to the efforts of Muriel and Billy Silk who have run the Jolly Fisherman for the past six years. A very varied menu is available, but you really should try sampling the fresh salmon or crab dishes which are inevitably the specialities. The highlight, and the most popular dish of all, is the crab meat soup made with fresh cream and whisky - it is to be

highly recommended. Billy spent twenty years as a local fisherman so there isn't much he doesn't know about selecting the very finest seafood available. In addition to serving excellent food, behind the bar they also stock a range of fine beers and there is always a real ale on tap often from a local brewery. Open all year with reduced opening hours in winter.

THE TANKERVILLE ARMS

Eglingham, Northumberland NE66 2TX
Tel: 01665 578444

The village of Eglingham lies on the B6346 between Alnwick and Wooler and here in this small village the only public house to be found is **The Tankerville Arms**. Built in the early 1700s this was originally a coaching house and today, the attractive stone exterior has a great olde worlde charm and appears very inviting.

The main bar area was probably once a barn and still features the original oak beams and stone flagged floor. There is also a lounge bar, seating 30 and separate 40-seater restaurant. Run by John Blackmore, his classic training as a chef has resulted in the superb quality of the food that is presented by the kitchens. There is a selection of bar meals served at lunch time and evenings, with a daily changing specials board as well as a special menu. The Tankerville Arms is also open for Sunday lunch. The dishes have a distinct French influence and you can expect to see game, poultry, steaks and sea food featured - many ingredients being sourced locally. The dessert menu is probably the highlight, so it is worth pacing yourself to be sure of doing it justice. Behind the bar there is a choice of real ales with the guest beers being changed every week. To the rear of the pub there is a huge beer garden with plenty of seating. In summer there is often a barbecue and customers are invited to cook their own! Regular live entertainment is arranged with quiz and theme nights - ring for details. There is no accommodation available at present but some is planned to be ready for 2002.

Lobster Pots, Craster

with Northumbrians for many years. The park includes Ladyburn Lake, where there is sailing and windsurfing, plus a visitors centre and picnic area. Before it became a park in 1989, the whole area was a huge open cast coal mine. The park is managed by Northumberland County Council. Nearby are the ruins of medieval **Chibburn Preceptory**, which belonged to the Knights Hospitaller.

with the Grey family who have produced many famous public figures - most notably the 2nd Earl Grey, the great social reformer and tea enthusiast. The gardens are open to the public in spring and summer and are noted for their beauty.

Craster Quarry closed in 1939, and is now a small nature reserve called the **Arnold Memorial Site**, managed by the Northumberland Wildlife Trust. It was this quarry that supplied London and other large cities with its kerbstones.

DRURIDGE BAY
12 miles SE of Alnwick off the A1068

Druridge Bay Country Park sits on an area of coastline that has been popular

Druridge Bay

EDLINGHAM
5 miles SW of Alnwick on the B6341

Edlingham mustn't be confused with the villages of Eglingham and Ellingham, both a few miles to the north. Here at Edlingham the moorland road crosses **Corby's Crags** where there is one of the finest views in Northumberland. The panorama encompasses the Cheviot Hills in the north, and to the south a rolling landscape of heather moors and crags stretches to Hadrian's Wall. The high tops of the North Pennines can even be glimpsed on a clear day.

Edlingham Castle was built in the 12th century but abandoned in 1650 when parts of it collapsed. The ruins were originally thought to be of a simple Northumbrian tower house, but excavations in the late 1970s and early 1980s showed that it as much more substantial than that. It is owned by English Heritage, and is open to the public.

EGLINGHAM
6 miles NW of Alnwick on the B6346

St Maurice's Church in this attractive village dates from about 1200, and was built on a site granted to the monks of

THE SHIP INN

Low Newton by the Sea,
Northumberland
Tel: 01665 576262

Enjoying an unrivalled position literally within yards of the beach, in the village of Low Newton-by-the-Sea, stands **The Ship Inn**. The pub is within a courtyard of cottages, all arranged in an open ended square around a small green, and this is all there is of the village! All the buildings are of stone and date back to the late 18th century, when they were originally built as fishermen's cottages, and most are now owned by the National Trust. Sadly, no fishing takes place from here now though the area is popular with visitors exploring the coastline and visiting the nearby National Trust owned nature reserve.

The Ship is open daily serving refreshing drinks and tasty home cooked food in a traditional, cosy atmosphere. Behind the bar they stock the usual main brands of beer and lager, together with the expected selection of spirits and soft drinks. The quality of the food is excellent with the menu utilising fresh local meat and fish where possible. The menu is regularly changed to make the most of seasonal produce and there is always a reasonable choice of dishes. However, don't expect to see the usual lasagne and chips, the dishes are much more interesting than that! Food is served each lunchtime, but phone for evening opening times out of season.

Lindisfarne in AD738 by King Ceowulf of Northumbria. In 1596 it was attacked by the Scots, and part of the chancel had to be rebuilt in the early 17th century.

A few bumps in a field not far away indicates where the village once stood, and a mile to the SW is a small hill fort with the quaint name of **The Ringses**.

Corby Crag, Edlingham

Dunstanburgh Castle

ELLINGHAM
7 miles N of Alnwick off the A1

Ellingham (pronounced "Ellin-jam") is a small agricultural village centred around **St Maurice's Church**, whose Norman details were all but swept away in a restoration of 1862. It features a central tower instead of the more usual west one. **Ellingham Hall** stands at the end of a quiet lane beyond the village.

EMBLETON
5 miles NE of Alnwick on the B1339

The dramatic ruins of **Dunstanburgh Castle** stand on a cliff top east of the village, on a site that was originally an Iron Age fort. The fabric of the castle as seen today was built in 1313 by Thomas, Earl of Lancaster, and in the Wars of the Roses it withstood a siege from troops led by Margaret of Anjou, Henry VI's Queen. The damage caused by the siege was never repaired, and the castle remains ruinous to this day.

The castle can't be reached by road, but a path from the village passing through Dunstan Steads, a mile south east of Embleton, will bring you to it. The castle, plus the whole coastline to the north as far as Brunton Burn is owned by the National Trust.

To the north of Embleton is the village of **Newton-by-the-Sea**, where, at Newton Seahouses, there are some attractive 18th century fisherman's cottages built round three sides of a square.

LONGFRAMLINGTON
9 miles SW of Alnwick on the A697

Longframlington owes part of its name to its principal family, the de Framlingtons, who are recorded as the 12th-century benefactors of Brinkburn Priory. The route of the **Devil's Causeway**, a Roman road between Hadrian's Wall and the Scottish border, can easily be traced west of the village,

Longstone House Hotel

182 Main Street, North Sunderland, Seahouses,
Northumberland NE68 7UP
Tel: 01665 720212 Fax: 01665 720211

The Longstone House Hotel is situated in the quiet, old part of Seahouses, which is called North Sunderland. It is only a few minutes away from miles of Heritage Coastline which carries the Blue Flag Award for clean beaches. Nearby is the picturesque fishing harbour of Seahouses, from where one can take boat trips to visit the bird sanctuaries and seal colonies of the Farne Islands. Owned and personally run by Judy Oxley and her family the hotel is named after the **'Longstone Lighthouse'**, home of the famous Grace Darling which can be visited on one of the many boat trips from Seahouses.

The hotel is English Tourist Board '2 star' standard commended with two bars; the Bamburgh Bar with a pool room, darts etc.; and the Lindisfarne Lounge which is a comfortable lounge bar where there is a log burner on cold days and evenings. Bar meals are available and there is also a restaurant - both serve a range of freshly prepared dishes based upon the traditional fine foods of Northumberland. The friendly clientele and staff make for a relaxing and pleasant atmosphere. There are eighteen bedrooms - double, single, twin bedded and family rooms as well as one 2 bedroomed Family Suite - all of which are en suite with either a bath and/or shower. Rooms are comfortable with central heating, tea and coffee facilities and colour televisions.

The area has a wide range of activities for the outdoor enthusiast with superb beaches, birdwatching, horse-riding (special riding breaks and limited stabling is available if booked in advance), sailing, diving, hiking, golfing (there are 8 golf courses within 25 miles of the hotel, special rates are available), tennis, sea & river fishing. Judy is always happy to advise you when planning your day having a wealth of knowledge of the area.

The Masons Arms

3 Dial Place, Warkworth,
Northumberland NE65 0UR
Tel: 01665 711398
Fax: 01665 711398

On the main street in the centre of Warkworth the delightful **Masons Arms** is housed within one of the oldest buildings in the town. Originally dating back to the early 1600s it became an ale house in 1715 and has provided refreshment to the locals and visitors to the area ever since. The charming exterior is white painted and gaily adorned with planted tubs, window boxes and hanging baskets throughout the year. The interior is cosy and inviting and has a very friendly and relaxing atmosphere. The large premises comprises a lounge and a public bar, divided by a long bar. Food is served each lunch time and evening, and children are welcome to join their parents for a meal. The menu offers a good choice of traditional dishes ranging from light snacks to hearty meals. All are freshly prepared and cooked on the premises and use local produce where possible. Behind the bar they reputedly sell the cheapest drinks in town, a claim which would certainly be worth checking out! They stock a good range of beer and lager with a selection of real ales also on tap. The owner Gary Rooney is a Geordie and brings a lot of humour to the over-bar chat ensuring that the Masons Arms is a well-liked pub. He organises a regular quiz night, occasional drinks promotions and there is a large screen TV for watching major sporting events.

along what is now a farm lane past Framlington Villa.

There are few shops here but the village retains the traditional craftsmanship of a Northumbrian pipe maker. The workshop, where you can see the production of these unique and beautiful musical instruments, is open to the public.

SEAHOUSES
13 miles NE of Alnwick on the B1340

Seahouses is a fishing port and small resort, strategically situated for viewing the Farne Islands. They lie between two and five miles off the coast, and boat trips are available to see them at close hand. Here too, you will find an interesting harbour, magnificent beaches and sand dunes stretching for miles on either side of the town.

WARKWORTH
6 miles S of Alnwick on the A1068

At the southern end of Alnmouth Bay, on the River Coquet, lies Warkworth, one of the grand castles that so distinguish this coast. The site has been fortified since the Iron Age, though the first stone castle was probably built by one "Roger, son of Richard", who had been granted the castle by Henry 11 in the 12th century.

What can be seen now is mainly late 12th and 13th century, including the great Carrickfergus Tower and the West Postern Towers, built by Roger's son, Robert. It came into the ownership of the Percys in 1332, in whose ownership it remained until comparatively recent times.

History was created 1399 when the Percys, including the most famous of

THE JACKDAW RESTAURANT AND GALLERY

34 Castle Street, Warkworth, Northumberland NE65 0UN
Tel: 01665 711488

Situated on the main street is the **Jackdaw Restaurant and Gallery**. This fine building is steeped in history and is believed to have been constructed in 1717 from local stone with a slate and pantile roof. The building is exceedingly well preserved and is decorated with colourful displays of hanging baskets in the summer months. The interior is equally fine with the original beamed ceilings and inglenook fireplace having been preserved. The traditional feel has been reflected in the mahogany furniture and Sanderson fabrics that have been used in the decor with the windows looking out on to the private garden to the rear.

Offering a cosy dining area, the Jackdaw has been owned and personally run by Rupert and Gillian Bell since 1984 and together they have built up the fine reputation that it now enjoys. Offering the very best in high quality home cooking, all the dishes are freshly prepared and served to order. The specialities include local beef, lamb and fish including Tweed smoked salmon.

In addition to the restaurant, we also have a fine selection of gifts including Royal Worcester, Limoges china

miniatures, greetings cards, limited edition prints and a good variety of produce, preserves and chocolates. This wonderful attraction has to be at the top of your list of places to visit when in the area.

BUSTON FARM HOLIDAY COTTAGES

Low Buston Hall, Warkworth, Morpeth, Northumberland NE65 0XY
Tel: 01665 714805   Fax: 01665 711345

The tiny village of Low Buston can be found in the narrow lanes just north and slightly inland of Warkworth. **Buston Farm** is a working arable farm comprising over 1000 acres of this delightful part of rural Northumberland. Jo Park is the daughter of the family that own and run the farm, and she is responsible for the self-catering holiday cottages. There are five in total, of varying sizes, and all have been recently refurbished and updated to provide every comfort for the modern holiday maker. The cottages vary in size and would suit a family, group of friends or a couple looking for a quiet escape.

Within the farm grounds are three stone built terraced cottages, sleeping four or five, and the much larger Butlesdon House which sleeps eight. Guests within Butlesdon House can also enjoy the colourful gardens, which are clearly well loved and carefully maintained, and garden furniture is available in the summer months. The fifth property is a cosy bungalow located at Low Newton by the Sea, about ten miles further along the coast. The convenient location of this area, just off the A1, makes these cottages an ideal base for touring the whole of the Northumberland region.

THE ORCHID ROOM COFFEE SHOP

Sanderson Arcade, Morpeth,
Northumberland NE61 1NS
Tel: 01670 511717

In the centre of the small market town of Morpeth, just off the main street, you will find the Sanderson Arcade. Incorporating a variety of small shops, there is here a most delightful cafe in the form of **The Orchid Room Coffee Shop**. Well established in a prime location within the arcade, this establishment has been run by Len and Joan Wedderburn for over seven years. The corner site is distinctive, with the frontage being painted a bright green. Inside there is seating for up to 45, with the light and airy decor being enhanced by a profusion of house plants, while an intimate atmosphere is created by the small lamps casting a rosy glow over each table. Popular with the locals, this is an ideal place to visit for some refreshment if you are exploring the town.

Open Monday to Saturday from 9.30-16.30, you can enjoy coffee, tea, soft drinks, home made cakes and scones as well as a range of snacks, soup and light lunches. Everything is freshly made and home baked under the supervision of Joan Wedderburn. This is easily the best coffee shop in the town with a friendly service being provided by neatly presented waitresses. In addition to the Orchid Room, Len and Joan also operate a popular sandwich bar which is attached.

River Coquet, Warkworth

them all, Harry - known as Hotspur - were instrumental in placing Henry Bolingbroke on the throne as Henry IV. The castle is now in the care of English Heritage and is a delightful sight in spring when the grass mound on which it stands is covered with thousands of daffodils.

Unusual and interesting is the walk to **The Hermitage**, along the riverside footpath below the castle, where a ferry takes you across the river to visit the tiny chapel hewn out of the solid rock. It dates from medieval times and was in use until late in the 16th century.

Warkworth is an interesting and beautiful village in its own right. An imposing fortified gatehouse on the 14th-century bridge, now only used by pedestrians, would enable an invading

army to be kept at bay north of the Coquet. **St Lawrence's Church** is almost wholly Norman, though its spire - an unusual feature on medieval churches in Northumberland - dates from the 14th century.

MORPETH

Morpeth, now Northumberland's county town, seems a long way from the mining areas further down the Wansbeck, both in spirit and appearance. It was a stopping point on the A1 from Newcastle and Edinburgh, and some fine inns were established.

The first of Morpeth's castles was Norman, and stood in what is now Carlisle Park. It was destroyed by William Rufus in 1095. The second was built close by, but was destroyed by King John in 1215. It was subsequently rebuilt, but was destroyed yet again by Montrose in 1644, though substantial ruins remain. The third - which isn't really a castle but has all the appearance of one - was built by John Dobson in 1828 as the county gaol and courthouse. It still stands.

The **Town Hall** was built to designs by Vanbrugh, and a handsome bridge over the Wansbeck was designed by Telford. The **Clock Tower** in the middle of Oldgate has been heightened several times. It probably dates from the early 17th century, though medieval stone was used in its construction. In its time it has served as a gaol and a place from where the nightly curfew was sounded. Its bells were a gift from a Major Main, who was elected MP for the town in 1707. He had intended them

Lindon Hall, Morpeth

for Berwick, but they didn't elect him, so, as a local saying goes, "the bells of Berwick still ring at Morpeth". The Clock Tower is one of only a handful of such buildings in England.

Somewhere not to be missed is the 13th century **Morpeth Chantry** on Bridge Street, close to the bridges over the Wansbeck. Originally the Chapel of All Saints, it has been in its time a cholera hospital, a mineral water factory and a school where the famous Tudor botanist William Turner was educated. Nowadays it houses a museum of the Northumbrian bagpipe, a musical instrument that is unique to the county, There is also a tourist information centre, a silversmiths and a mountain sports shop.

St Mary's Church, lying to the south of the river, dates from the 14th century. In the churchyard is the grave of **Emily Davison**, the suffragette who was killed

under the hooves of "Anmer", the king's horse, during the Derby of 1913. He funeral attracted thousands of people to Morpeth. About a mile west of the town are the scant remains of **Newminster Abbey**, a Cistercian foundation dating from the 12th century. It was founded by monks from Fountains Abbey in Yorkshire.

AROUND MORPETH

ASHINGTON
5 miles W of Morpeth on the A197

Ashington is a sprawling town around the River Wansbeck, built to serve the mining industry, and now has modern shopping centres, swimming baths and leisure centres. The two-mile-long **Wansbeck Riverside Park**, which has been developed along the embankment,

THE BLACKSMITH'S COFFEE SHOP

Belsay, Newcastle NE20 0DU
Tel: 01661 881024
Fax: 01661 881103

In the heart of the pretty village of Belsay, **The Blacksmith's Coffee Shop** enjoys a prime site and can be easily located by visitors to the area. The building has origins in the mid-1800s and in 1930 became a new and impressive blacksmith's shop for an Edwin Greer who at the time was reputed to be the finest blacksmith in Northumberland. It was in 1990 that Anne and Jo Atkinson converted it into the popular, elegant tea room that visitors find today. A mother and

daughter team, Anne and Jo have worked hard to establish the reputation that The Blacksmith's enjoys both with the locals and the many visitors, with both ladies tending tables, working in the kitchen or at their other coffee shop in Belsay.

The main selling point is the freshness of the food served, with everything from the bread to the ham being cooked on the premises. The menu offers a good range of old-fashioned, home cooked dishes that is rarely found these days. Visitors can enjoy simply a cup of tea, or a full cooked lunch, with all dishes being freshly prepared to order. The main restaurant area is bright and airy while also being comfortable and relaxing with the bare stone walls adding to the ambience. The service is efficient, with the staff being friendly and attentive. Open Tuesday-Sunday.

offers sailing and angling facilities, plus a four mile walk along the mouth of the River Wansbeck. The famous footballing brothers Bobby and Jackie Charlton were born in Ashington in the 1930s.

BEDLINGTON
5 miles SE of Morpeth off the A189

Bedlington was formerly known as the county town of Bedlingtonshire, a district of the County Palatinate of Durham until it was incorporated into Northumberland in 1844. It became the centre of a prosperous mining and iron-founding community and has two important links with railway history. It was the town in which the rolled-iron rails for the Stockton and Darlington Railway were manufactured, and also the birthplace of the great locomotive engineer, Sir Daniel Gooch, one of the greatest engineers of his day. He was the locomotive superintendent on the Great Western Railway, and the man who first linked up North America and Europe via a telegraph line.

The town gave its name to a breed of dog, the Bedlington terrier. There is an attractive country park at **Humford Mill**, with an information centre and nature trails. At **Plessey Woods**, south west of the town, another country park extends along the wooded banks of the River Blyth, around Plessey Mill, with trails and a Visitor Centre.

Near Bomarsund, close to Bedlington, is **Earth Balance 2000**, a 260 acre visitor attraction that examines environmental issues. There are eco-buildings, a maze, a nature reserve and even a pub that brews its own beer.

BELSAY
7 miles SW of Morpeth on the A696

Belsay Hall was built for Sir Charles Monck on an estate that already had a

Belsay Castle

BELSAY HALL CASTLE AND GARDENS
Belsay, near Ponteland, Northumberland NE20 0DX
Tel: 01661 881297 Fax: 01661 881043

Why not indulge yourself by visiting one of the best English Heritage properties in the area - **Belsay Hall Castle and Gardens**? The hall was built for Sir Charles Monck on an estate that already had a castle and Jacobean mansion, and they all stand in 30 beautiful acres of landscaped gardens. There's a magnolia garden, terraces, rhododendrons, a winter garden and croquet lawn, and a quarry garden. The whole estate has been listed as Grade 1 in the Register of gardens. In addition there's free parking, a tearoom (summer only) and various small exhibitions. Opening Times: Open all year; 1 April -30 September 10.00-18.00; 1 October 10.00-17.00; 1 November-31 March 10.00-16.00; closed 24-26 December and 1 January; Admission charge

Wallington Estate

SHOULDER OF MUTTON

East Road, Longhorsley,
Northumberland NE65 8SY
Tel: 01670 788236

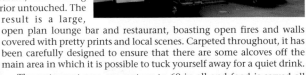

The Shoulder of Mutton is a large and impressive establishment which can be found in the village of Longhorsley on the main A697 Morpeth to Coldstream road. Dating back to the 18th century, the structure has been transformed to create a large and comfortable pub and restaurant, while leaving the original, characterful exterior untouched. The result is a large,

open plan lounge bar and restaurant, boasting open fires and walls covered with pretty prints and local scenes. Carpeted throughout, it has been carefully designed to ensure that there are some alcoves off the main area in which it is possible to tuck yourself away for a quiet drink.

The restaurant area can seat up to 60 in all and food is served all day, seven days a week. The menu offers an impressive selection of traditional dishes, all freshly cooked and sensibly priced. The speciality of the house is the game dishes with duck and pheasant being regularly featured, when in season. The bar stocks a choice of cask ales which are varied regularly. There is a beer garden to the rear of the building which is popular in summer months.

The Shoulder of Mutton has excellent access and facilities for disabled and less mobile customers, with easy direct access from the main car park.

castle and Jacobean mansion (see panel on page 125). Two miles west is the **Bolam Lake Country Park**, with a 25 acre lake (suitable for coarse fishing and canoeing), paths and picnic areas. It is owned by Northumberland County Council.

LONGHORSLEY
6 miles N of Morpeth off the A697

Longhorsley is noted for being the home of Thomas Bell, inventor of self-raising flour. He called it Bell's Royal, which was later changed to Bero.

Though born at Blackheath in London, Emily Davison spent a lot of time in the village. A plaque on the wall of the post office, her former home, commemorates her death under the feet of the king's horse at Epsom in 1913. Her suffragette activities are remembered by the local Women's Institute each year when flowers are placed on her grave in Morpeth.

NEWBIGGIN BY THE SEA
7 miles E of Morpeth on the A197

Newbiggin by the Sea is a fishing village and small resort enjoying an attractive stretch of coastline with rocky inlets and sandy beaches, now much improved after the ravages of the coal industry. **St Bartholomew's Church** has a particularly interesting 13th century interior. The village has the oldest operational lifeboat house in Britain. It was built in 1851.

WALLINGTON HALL
11 miles W of Morpeth off the B6342

Wallington Hall, lying deep in the heart of the Northumbrian countryside, is a National Trust property dating from 1688. The two great families associated with the place - the Blacketts and the Trevelyans - have each made their own mark on what must be one of the most elegant houses in Northumberland. In

Wallington Hall

Wallington Great Hall

WOODHORN
6 miles E of Morpeth on the A197

At Woodhorn, close to Ashington, there is the fascinating late-Anglo-Saxon **St Mary's Church**, said to be the oldest church building in Northumberland. The outside was heavily restored in 1843, though the inside is almost wholly pre-Norman. There is a 13th century effigy of Agnes de Velence, wife of Hugh de Baliol, brother of the Scottish king, John Baliol. The **Woodhorn Colliery Museum**, which is linked to the **Queen Elizabeth Country Park** by a short light railway, offers interesting displays of mining and the social history of the area (see panel below).

the Great Hall is a famous collection of paintings about Northumbrian history, and one of the rooms has an unusual collection of doll's houses.

Nearby is the village of **Cambo**, where Lancelot Brown, also known as Capability Brown, was born.

WOODHORN COLLIERY MUSEUM AND QEII COUNTRY PARK RAILWAY

QEII Country park, Ashington, Northumberland
Tel: 01670 856968

If you want to explore the history of mining in the Wansbeck area of Northumberland, then the **Woodhorn Colliery Museum** is for you. Set in the QE11 Country Park, it has the reputation of being one of the best local museums in the country. It's stunning interactive exhibition called "Turning the Pages" on the Lindisfarne Gospels recently won it a coveted Interpret Britain Award. Through the park runs the narrow-gauge QEII Country Park Railway, which is always popular with children. There's also a cafe, gift shop and ample parking. Opening times: Open all year from Wednesday to Sunday and on bank holidays (plus Mondays from June 26-August 21); May-August 10.00-17.00; September-April 10.00-16.00; Free

6 Southern Northumberland

Most of the area inland from the north bank of the Tyne was, like its neighbour on the south bank, part of the former county of Tyne and Wear, which has now disappeared as an administrative unit. It's mostly built up, though there are still areas of rural calm and beauty. Dominating it all is Newcastle-upon-Tyne, one of Britain's most important cities. It's built up area stretches out as far as the small

Tyne Bridges

towns of Tynemouth and Whitley Bay to the east, Longbenton to the north and Throckley to the west.

Industry made this area. It is real Geordie country, steeped in hard work and Newcastle Brown Ale. People found employment in coalmines, great engineering works and shipyards, and didn't travel far to spend their leisure time or holidays. They headed for Whitley Bay or Tynemouth, eight miles east of Newcastle city centre on the North Sea coast, but a lifetime away from their harsh living and working conditions. Or they could head north into rural Northumberland, one of Britain's most beautiful and unspoilt counties.

Tyne Valley

Away from Newcastle there is grandeur and history as well. Seaton Delavel Hall, near Seaton Sluice, is a grand mansion in the Palladian style, designed by Vanbrugh for Admiral George Delavel. Prudhoe, which is south of the Tyne but in Northumberland, has its castle, dating from the 12th century, which was laid siege to in 1174 by William the Lion of Scotland. At Wylam, west of Newcastle, was born one of the North East's greatest sons - George Stephenson. And in Wallsend - so called

The Castle, Newcastle upon Tyne

because this was where Hadrian's Wall ended - there's the Stephenson Railway Museum.

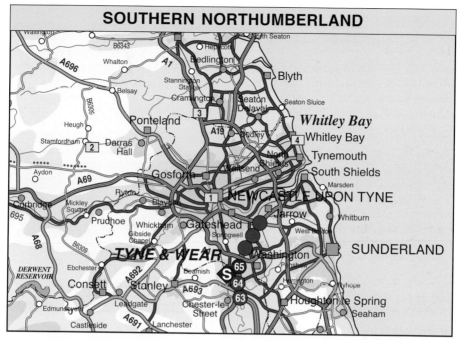

SOUTHERN NORTHUMBERLAND

Wallington · B6343 · North Seaton · Heppscott · Bedlington · Whalton · A1 · A696 · Stannington Station · Blyth · Belsay · Cramlington · Seaton Delaval · Seaton Sluice · B6305 · Heugh · Ponteland · A19 · Whitley Bay · Stamfordham · Darras Hall · Rudley · Whitley Bay · Aydon · A69 · Gosforth · North Shields · Tynemouth · Wallsend · South Shields · Ryton · Blaydon · NEWCASTLE UPON TYNE · Marsden · Corbridge · Mickley Square · 695 · Prudhoe · Whickham · Gateshead · Jarrow · Whitburn · Gibside Chapel · Springwell · West Boldon · A68 · B6309 · TYNE & WEAR · Washington · SUNDERLAND · DERWENT RESERVOIR · Ebchester · A692 · Beamish · Penshaw · Herrington · Ryhope · Consett · Stanley · A693 · Houghton le Spring · Leadgate · Chester-le-Street · Seaham · Edmundbyers · A691 · Castleside · Lanchester

© MAPS IN MINUTES ™ (1999)

PLACES TO STAY, EAT, DRINK AND SHOP

1	The International Centre for Life, Newcastle upon Tyne	Visitor centre on the secrets of life	page 134
2	The Stamfordham Bay Horse Inn, Stamfordham	Pub, food and accommodation	page 137
3	The Coffee Shop, Blagdon	Coffee shop and restaurant	page 138
4	St Mary's Lighthouse, Whitley Bay	Lighthouse and visitor centre	page 140

NEWCASTLE-UPON-TYNE

Newcastle, the region's capital, is one of Britain's most exciting cities, and contains many magnificent public buildings and churches. Situated above the River Tyne, it is linked to its neighbour Gateshead by a series of road and rail bridges.

The most impressive is the **New Tyne Road Bridge**, commonly known as the "coat hanger bridge". This has become the icon by which Newcastle is internationally known, and was opened in 1928. It bears an uncanny resemblance to the Sydney Harbour Bridge, which isn't surprising - both were designed by the same firm of civil engineers.

Newcastle was, and is, many things - a Roman frontier station, a medieval fortress town with a "new" castle built in the 11th century, an ecclesiastical centre, a great port, a mining, engineering and shipbuilding centre and a focal point of the Industrial Revolution that changed the face of the world.

And, thanks to the **Metro Rapid Transport System**, the city and its

surroundings are closely linked. It is the second largest underground rail network in Britain, though, like the London Underground, Britain's largest, most out of town portions are above ground. The system takes in South Shields and

Tyne Bridges

Gateshead south of the city, and goes as far east as Tynemouth and Whitley Bay north of the Tyne. It even links up with Newcastle International Airport, and it takes a mere 20 minutes to go from the airport to the city centre - the shortest time of any city centre-airport link in Europe. In 2001, the system will be extended as far as Sunderland, 15 miles away, to create a truly regional network that can compete with some of the major underground and rapid transport systems in Europe.

The Quayside is the first view of Newcastle for visitors from the south, whether travelling by road or rail. This area is the symbolic and historic heart of this elegant city and boasts 17th-century merchants' houses mingling

Metro Rapid Transport System

with Georgian and classical Victorian architecture. The area has been revitalised in recent years with some sensitive and imaginative restoration of the river front area. There are now a number of lively cafes and wine bars, with craft stalls and street entertainers as well. This is also the venue for a regular Sunday market.

The **Castle Keep** at Castle Garth was started by Henry II in the 12th century on the site of the "new castle" which gave the city its name, with King John completing the work. This earlier new castle was probably made of wood, and was built by Robert, eldest son of William 1, in 1080 on the site of a Roman fort called Pons Aelius. This is thought to have been the start of Hadrian's Wall before it was extended east. The wooden castle was built after uprisings against the new Norman overlords, and after the killing of Bishop Walcher in Gateshead at a meeting to discuss local grievances.

Henry's massive new structure was built entirely of stone, and reached 100 feet in height. Although the battlements and turrets were added in the 19th century, most of it is Norman. The only other remaining castle building is **Black Gate**, dating from 1247 onwards. If at first glance the structure looks a little unusual, it is because of the house built on top of it in the 17th century. The castle was in use during the Civil War, when it was taken by the Scottish army after the Royalist defeat at the Battle of Newburn, five miles west of Newcastle, in 1640.

Many of the other medieval buildings were demolished in the mid 19th century to make way for the railway, and the Castle and Black Gate were almost demolished as well. Today the main Scotland rail line runs between the two, and the London branch passes to

Central Arcade

the west of the Castle Keep before crossing the river over the High Level Bridge.

Newcastle was at one time surrounded by stout walls that were in places 20 to 30 feet high and seven feet thick. Parts of these survive and include a number of small towers which were built at regular intervals. Begun in 1265, the walls were eventually completed in the mid-14th century. They were described as having a "strength and magnificence" which "far passeth all the walls of the cities of England and most of the cities of Europe". The best remaining section is the **West Walls** behind Stowell Street. Another good section is between Forth Street and Hanover Street, south of Central Station. This leads you to spectacular views of the River Tyne from the "Hanging Gardens of Hanover Street" perched on the cliff side.

THE INTERNATIONAL CENTRE FOR LIFE

Times Square, Newcastle upon Tyne NE1 4EP
Tel:0191 243 8200 Fax: 0191 243 8201
Website: www.lifeinteractiveworld.co.uk
Email: general@centre-for-life.co.uk

This spectacular new visitor centre, which cost
over £70 million and covers ten acres, has a
unique purpose - it wants to study the secrets
of life, and open them up to everyone. It takes
you on a trip through four billion years, from
when life started on earth to the present day.
During the trip, you'll experience magical 3D
shows, live theatre, film, sound, light and
audience participation. Plus you'll be learning
about life itself - what it is, how it functions,
and how it equips itself to survive. You'll learn
about single cell creatures, DNA, forensic science, senses such as smell, taste and sight, and so much
more.

The International Centre for Life has many aspects. There's a Bioscience Centre, an Institute of
Human Genetics (part of Newcastle University), a Life Lab, Times Square (the largest open square to
be created in Newcastle for over 100 years), and the amazing Life Interactive World. This is divided

into eight zones, each one highlighting an
aspect of human development. Zone one,
for instance, introduces you to evolution,
zone two deals with DNA, which are the
building blocks of life, Zone three deals with
cells, and so on until we reach zone nine,
when we experience an amusement arcade
of the future! Here visitors can test their co-
ordination and reflexes - two of the basic
skills which keep creatures alive in a hostile
world! This is science presented in an
imaginative and stimulating way. The most
scary zone must surely be zone eight, where
life is shown to be a roller coaster, using
the world's longest continual motion ride.

But all aspects of Life Interactive World
are entertaining and fun, and visitor

sometimes never realise that as they experience
what's on offer, they're learning as well! Which
brings us to the brain. Zone six deals with our
most important organ, and we can actually step
inside a huge one, and follow a day in the life
of a typical North East family. The Centre is the
first time anywhere in the world that science,
biotechnology, research, education,
entertainment and ethics have been brought
together on a single site. It's right in the centre
of Newcastle, next to Central Station and a stop
on the Metro. Within Times Square there are
shops (including a souvenir shop), a restaurant
and a cafe.

Opening times: 10.00-17.00 every day except
Christmas day and New Year's Day; Admission
charge

One unusual feature of the walls was that they passed right through the grounds of the monastery of the Black Friars, or Dominicans, which caused the prior to protest loudly. To keep the peace, a door was cut through to allow the monks to reach their orchards and gardens, and the monastery was given a key to it.

Newcastle has two cathedrals - the Anglican **St Nicholas's Cathedral** on St Nicholas Street, and the Roman Catholic **St Mary's Cathedral** in Clayton West Street. St Nicholas, dating from the 14th and 15th centuries, was formerly the city's parish church, and it still has all the feel of an intimate parish church about it. St Mary's was designed by Pugin, and opened in 1842. The spire he designed was never built, the present one dating from 1872.

The city centre is compact, lying mostly within about a square mile, so it is easy to explore. For the most part the streets are wide and spacious and, like the later **Quayside** developments after the great fire of 1855, much of the architecture is in the Classical style. The focal point is Earl Grey's monument of 1838 which stands at the head of Grey Street about which John Betjeman wrote "not even Regent Street in London, can compare with that subtle descending curve."

During the 17th and early 18th centuries, Newcastle was a major coal port, with its core - still basically medieval in layout - near the riverside. But by the late 1700s the city began moving north, and in the early 1800s architects like William Newton, John Stokoe and John Dobson began designing some elegant Georgian buildings and spacious squares.

This is the core of modern day Newcastle, a city that is renowned for its shopping. In fact, **Eldon Square** is one of the largest city shopping centres in Europe, and contains department stores, restaurants, pubs and cafes, bus and Metro stations, and a sports and recreation centre. The adjoining Eldon Garden is smaller, with a number of specialist shops. A little further out is **Blackfriars**, a former Dominican monastery dating from 1239. It was earmarked for demolition in the 1960s, but was eventually saved. The church is long gone, but the rest has now been renovated and opened as a craft centre

Blackfriars Complex

and restaurant grouped around a small square. It's another of the area's hidden places, and well worth a visit.

This is a metropolitan city of great vibrancy and activity, and there's plenty to do, with a rich variety of entertainment on offer. There is a choice of theatres, cinemas, concerts and opera. The nightlife has quite a reputation too - the pubs are so popular that queues form to get into them on a Saturday night. In fact, the city was voted by an

American magazine as the eighth best place in the world to party. There are some fine restaurants too, with every type of cuisine on offer, and like many large cities there is a Chinatown.

The modern **Civic Centre** has won architectural awards, and there is a whole cluster of museums and art galleries, in fact, too many to describe them all in detail. There's the **Discovery Museum** (the North's largest museum complex), **Laing Art Gallery** on New Bridge Street (with its **Proctor and Gamble Children's Gallery**), **The International Centre for Life** near Newcastle's main rail station (see panel on page 132), the **Hatton Gallery** at the Quadrangle, Newcastle University, the **Hancock Museum** at Barras Bridge, the **Museum of Antiquities** on King's Road, the **Trinity Maritime Centre** on Broad Chare, the **Military Museum** at Exhibition Park, and the **Newburn Hall Motor Museum** at Townfield Gardens in Newburn, on the western edge of the city, to name some of the best-known.

And down near the quayside is a unique group of half-timbered houses known as **Bessie Surtees House**, owned by English Heritage. The rooms are richly decorated with elaborate plaster ceilings, and there is some beautiful 17th century wall panelling.

To the west, on the south bank of the Tyne, is **Blaydon**, famous for its races, which inspired one of Newcastle's anthems - *"The Blaydon Races"*. But horse racing hasn't been held here since 1916, and the racecourse is no more. Gosforth, or more properly, High Gosforth, to the north of the city, is where horse racing now takes place. Near Blaydon is the **Path Head Water Mill**, a restored 18th century mill that can be visited (see panel on page 34).

Newcastle is more than just a regional centre. It's a northern capital - a proud city that doesn't look to the south (or to anywhere else, for that matter) for inspiration and guidance. It is one of the great cities of England, if not Europe, and such is its confidence that, with its neighbour Gateshead across the Tyne, it is bidding to become **European City of Culture** in the year 2008.

AROUND NEWCASTLE-UPON-TYNE

BLYTH
12 miles NE of Newcastle on the A193

Northumberland has one of the most romantically beautiful coastlines in all England, much of it totally unspoilt - but it has its contrasts too. The southeast corner of the county, between Blyth and Newbiggin, has an industrial heritage of coalmining in the Northumberland coal fields. This is an industry which has declined rapidly in recent years, a loss from which the area is only slowly recovering, but even this industrialised part of Northumberland has much to offer the visitor.

Blyth is a small industrial town at the mouth of the River Blyth. The oldest part is around an 18th century lighthouse called the **High Light**. The town claims its own piece of railway history with one of the country's earliest wagonways, the **Plessey Wagonway**, dating from the 17th century and built to carry coal from the pits to the riverside. As well as coal mining and shipbuilding, the town was once a centre of salt production, and in 1605 it is recorded that there were eight salt pans in Blyth.

But the area still has sandy beaches, one extending down to Seaton Sluice, the other to the north. The place was a submarine base during the Second World War, and is now the headquarters of the **Royal Northumberland Yacht Club**.

MICKLEY SQUARE
10 miles W of Newcastle on the A695

A signpost at Mickley Square points you to **Cherryburn**. The house is noted as the birthplace of Thomas Bewick, the well-known illustrator and engraver. It contains an exhibition of his woodcuts and there are frequent demonstrations of the printing techniques used in his time. It is owned by the National Trust.

George Stephenson's Birthplace, Wylam

PONTELAND
7 miles NW of Newcastle on the A696

Though this small town (pronounced "Pont-ee-land")has become a dormitory

THE STAMFORDHAM BAY HORSE INN

Stamfordham, Newcastle upon Tyne NE18 0PB
Tel: 01661 886244 Fax: 01661 886244
Or call free and ask for us
  by name on 0800 600900
e-mail stay@stamfordham-bay.co.uk
website www.stamfordham-bay.co.uk

The quiet village of Stamfordham is located just 12 miles northwest of Newcastle and easily located on the B6309 in an area that is full of historical interest. Popular with artists and photographers, the picturesque **Stamfordham Bay Horse Inn** enjoys an idyllic location on the village green and easily found even by first time

visitors to the area. The main structure of the attractive stone building dates from 1590 when it was probably originally a fortified farmhouse, although some parts are believed to date back even further.

Customers can enjoy a refreshing drink from the well-stocked bar with a good range of real ales, beer, lager and soft drinks being available. Food is served each lunchtime and evening, from a wide ranging menu of restaurant meals and bar snacks, and can be enjoyed in the cosy dining area. The dishes are mainly traditional English cuisine with some more exotic Oriental dishes to spice things up! The superb locally roasted coffee would round off any meal, and can also be enjoyed throughout the day.

Today's visitors will find this Grade II listed hostelry offering a warm and friendly welcome to customers old and new, with the present owners Eric and Linda Jordan taking great pride in the quality of service throughout. The clientele is of all ages, with regular customers drawn from the surrounding area and the city of Newcastle. Popular with day trippers, walkers and cyclists the bed and breakfast accommodation also makes this a popular choice with tourists. Conveniently situated as a touring base, or simply for a brief stop while touring the area, the Stamfordham Bay Horse is a perfect choice. There is a total of six, comfortably furnished, en-suite rooms provided - ring for full details.

for Newcastle-upon-Tyne, with a lot of recent development, it still has a character of its own. **St Mary's Church** - much altered, but essentially 12th century, stands opposite the attractive Blackbird Inn, housed in a 13th and 14th century fortified house. Within the gardens of the Old Vicarage is a 16th century vicar's pele.

A few miles north of Ponteland are **Kirkley Hall Gardens**, which are open to the public. There are 35,000 different species of labelled plant here, and it is home to the national collections of beech, dwarf willow and ivy.

Prudhoe Castle

PRUDHOE
9 miles W of Newcastle on the A695

The romantic ruins of **Prudhoe Castle** are in the care of English Heritage. It was unsuccessfully attacked by King William the Lion of Scotland in 1173

THE COFFEE SHOP

The Milkhope Centre, Blagdon, Seaton Burn, Newcastle
Tel: 01670 789878 Fax: 01661 881103

Just off the A1 eight miles north of Newcastle, you will find the **Milkhope Centre**. This is a relatively new development of some old buildings that at one time formed part of a country estate. The stone structure has a long frontage with some stunning period design features, including craftsman-made doors and windows, and although it is over 200 years old it looks like it was built only yesterday.

The complex comprises a number of high quality retail outlets and here visitors will also find **The Coffee Shop**, owned and run by Anne and Jo Atkinson who also run The Blacksmith's Coffee Shop in

Belsay. This is a relatively new venture, and the mother and daughter team are currently expanding into an adjoining unit to bring the total number of covers to 80.

Food is served each day from a menu offering a good range of home-cooked dishes catering to all tastes. Visitors can enjoy simply a cup of tea, or a full cooked lunch, with all dishes being freshly prepared to order. All the food served, from the bread to the delicious cakes, have been cooked on the premises. Open seven days a week.

Seaton Delaval Hall

drawbridge, a new gatehouse and a chapel. The oriel window above the altar of the chapel is thought to be one of the finest in England. A Georgian manor house in the courtyard houses an exhibition describing the history of the castle, and a video explaining the history of other castles in Northumberland.

SEATON SLUICE
8 miles NE of Newcastle on the A193

and 1174, and the threat of further attacks made Henry 11 agree to a new stone castle being built. When it was completed in the 12th century it was one of the finest in Northumberland, and was later provided with a moat and

Inland from Seaton Sluice is **Seaton Delaval Hall**, widely regarded as being one of the finest houses in the north of England. This superb Vanbrugh mansion, the ancestral home of the Delavals, was built in the Palladian style in the early 18th century for Admiral George Delaval, and although the building suffered from a series of damaging fires, extensive restoration has been carried out. In the grounds of the house stands the Norman **St Mary's Chapel**.

TYNEMOUTH AND WHITLEY BAY
8 miles E of Newcastle on the A193

These two towns form a linked resort. Overlooking the river at Tynemouth is the notable **Collingwood Monument**, the grand statue of Admiral Lord Collingwood, Nelson's second in command at Trafalgar, who went on to win the battle after Nelson's death. The four guns below the statue are from his ship, the "Royal Sovereign". **Tynemouth Priory** was built over the remains of a 7th-century monastery which was the burial place of St Oswin, king of Deira (the portion of Northumbria south of the Tees), who was murdered in 651. The

Seaton Delaval Hall

Whitley Bay

priory was as much a fortress as a monastery, which explains the existence of the adjoining 13th century castle ruins.

The Long Sands lead on past Cullercoats, an old fishing village, to the seaside resort of Whitley Bay. On a small island, easily reached on foot at low tide, is **St Mary's Lighthouse**, now converted into a museum and run by North Tyneside Council (see panel below). Visitors can climb the 137 steps to the top and get magnificent views of the Northumberland coast. The island is now a bird sanctuary. The town has some excellent, safe beaches.

WALLSEND AND NORTH SHIELDS
3 miles E of Newcastle on the A193

This was where Hadrian's Wall ended, at a fort called Segedunum. The two communities of Wallsend and North Shields are wedged between Tynemouth and Whitley Bay to the East and Newcastle to the west, and though the towns are not especially interesting, two attractions make the place worth a visit. One is the **Stephenson Railway Museum** in Middle Engine Lane, and the other is a reconstruction of **Segedunum Roman Fort** on Buddle Street.

George Stephenson began his career as a humble engine-man at Willington Ballast Hill, before moving to Killingworth where he eventually became engine-wright. He was the engineer on the world's first passenger rail line - the Stockton to Darlington

St Mary's Lighthouse

St Mary's Island, Whitley Bay NE26 4RS
Tel: 0191 200 8650 Fax: 0191 200 8654
Website: stmarys-lighthouse.ntb.org.uk

Just north of Whitley Bay, you'll find **St Mary's Lighthouse** and the adjoining keepers' cottages, situated on a small island which is accessible at low tide. It was built in 1898, and was closed down in 1984. Now it has been converted into a fascinating small museum and visitor centre by North Tyneside Council. There are 137 steps to the top, though the climb is

worth it - the views are spectacular! If the climb doesn't appeal, you can still see it courtesy of a video at ground level. An exhibition explains the history of the lighthouse and the varied wildlife of the island, which is a nature reserve. There's also a small souvenir shop, and plenty of parking on the mainland. Opening times: Depends on tides; phone for leaflet; Admission charge

railway, opened in 1825. The museum remembers the man and his achievements, as well as explaining railway history in the area.

Segedunum (which means "strong fort") stood at the eastern end of the Hadrian's Wall. Originally the wall only went as far as Newcastle, but it was decided to extend it to deter sea attacks. There are only scant remains of the structure in the district nowadays.

Segedunum is a reconstruction of what the Roman fort would have looked like. Over 600 Roman soldiers would have been garrisoned here at any one time, and the area must have been a bustling place. Now visitors can explore the reconstructed fort, get a stunning view from a 114-feet viewing tower, and watch archaeologists uncovering yet more foundations of the original wall.

List of
Tourist Information Centres

CLEVELAND

GUISBOROUGH

Priory Grounds, Church Street, Guisborough
Tel: (01287) 633801

HARTLEPOOL

Hartlepool Art Gallery & Information Centre,
Church Square, Hartlepool TS24 8EQ
Tel: (01429) 266522 Ext. 2407/2408

MIDDLESBROUGH

51 Corporation Road, Middlesborough
Tel: (01642) 243425/264330

SALTBURN

3 Station Buildings, Station Square,
Saltburn-by-the-Sea
Tel: (01287) 622422

STOCKTON

Theatre Yard, Off High Street,
Stockton-on-Tees TS18 1AT
Tel: (01642)615080

COUNTY DURHAM

BARNARD CASTLE

43 Galgate, Barnard Castle DL12 8AA
Tel: (01833) 690909

BEAMISH

The North of England Open Air Museum,
Beamish DH9 0RG
Tel: (0191) 3702533

Open during summer months only

BISHOP AUCKLAND

Town Hall,Market Place, Bishop Auckland
DL14 7NP
Tel: (01388) 604922

DARLINGTON

4 West Row, Darlington DL1 5PW
Tel: (01325) 382698

DURHAM CITY

Market Place, Durham City DH1 3NJ
Tel: (0191) 3843720

MIDDLETON-IN-TEESDALE

10 Market Place, Middleton-in-Teesdale
DL12 0QG
Tel: (01833) 641001

PETERLEE

20 The Upper Chare, Peterlee SR8 1BW
Tel: (0191) 5864450

STANHOPE

Durham Dales Centre, Castle Gardens,
Stanhope DL13 2FJ
Tel: (01388) 527650
Email: 100135.2517@compuserve.com

NORTHUMBERLAND

ADDERSTONE

Adderstone Services, Adderstone Garage,
Belford NE70 7JU
Tel: (01668) 213678

ALNWICK

The Shambles, Alnwick NE66 1TN
Tel: (01665) 510665

AMBLE

Council Sub Offices, Dilston Terrace, Amble
NE65 0DQ
Tel: (01665) 712313

Open during Summer months only

BELLINGHAM

Main Street, Bellingham, Hexham
NE48 2BQ
Tel: (01434) 220616

BERWICK UPON TWEED

Castlegate Car Park, Berwick upon Tweed
TD15 1BN
Tel: (01289) 330733

CORBRIDGE

Hill Street, Corbridge NE45 5AA
Tel: (01434) 632815

Open during the summer months only

CRASTER

Craster Car Park, Craster NE66 3TW
Tel: (01665) 576007

Open during the summer months only

HALTWHISTLE

Church Hall, Main Street, Haltwhistle
NE49 9HN
Tel: (01434) 322002

HEXHAM

Manor Office, Hallgate, Hexham
NE46 1QE
Tel: (01434) 605225

MORPETH

The Chantry, Bridge Street, Morpeth
NE61 1PJ
Tel: (01670) 511323

ONCE BREWED

Military Road, Bardon Mill, Hexham
NE47 7AN
Tel: (01434) 344396

Open during summer months only

OTTERBURN

Otterburn Mill Visitors Centre, Otterburn
NE19 1JT
Tel: (01830) 520093

PRUDHOE

Waterworld, Front Street, Prudhoe
NE24 5DQ
Tel: (01661) 833144

ROTHBURY

National Park Information Centre,
Church House, Church Street, Rothbury
NE65 7UP

Tel: (01669) 620887

Open during summer months only

SEAHOUSES

Car Park, Seafield Road, Seahouses
NE68 7SW

Tel: (01665) 720884

Open during summer months only

WOOLER

Bus Station Car Park, High Street, Wooler
NE71 6LQ

Tel: (01668) 281602

Open during summer months only

TYNE AND WEAR

GATESHEAD

Central Library, Prince Consort Road,
Gateshead NE8 4LN

Tel: (0191) 4773478

GATESHEAD METROCENTRE

Portcullis, 7 The Arcade, MetroCentre,
Gateshead NE11 9YL

Tel: (0191) 4606345

JARROW

Bedes World, Jarrow Hill, Church Bank,
Jarrow

Tel: (0191) 4892106

NEWCASTLE UPON TYNE

Central Library, Princess Square,
Newcastle upon Tyne NE1 5AF

Tel: (0191) 2610610

NEWCASTLE UPON TYNE

Main Concourse, Central Station,
Newcastle upon Tyne

Tel: (0191) 2300030

NEWCASTLE AIRPORT

Woolsington, Newcastle Upon Tyne
NE13 8BZ

Tel: (0191) 2144422/2860966 ext.4422

NORTH SHIELDS

International Ferry Terminal, Royal Quays,
North Shields NE29 6DW

Tel: (0191) 2005895

Open during summer months only

SOUTH SHIELDS

Museum and Art Gallery,Ocean Road,
South Shields NE33 2HZ

Tel: (0191) 4546612

SOUTH SHIELDS

Amphitheatre, Sea Road, South Shields
NE33 2LD

Tel: (0191) 4557411

Open during summer months only

SUNDERLAND

Unit 3, Crowtree Road, Sunderland
SR1 1RF

Tel: (0191) 5650990/565960

WHITLEY BAY

Park Road, Whitley Bay NE26 1EJ

Tel: (0191) 2008535

Index of Towns, Villages and Places of Interest

List of Advertisers

A

B

C

Hidden Places Order Form

To order any of our publications just fill in the payment details below and complete the order form *overleaf*. For orders of less than 4 copies please add £1 per book for postage and packing. Orders over 4 copies are P & P free.

Please Complete Either:

I enclose a cheque for £ [＿＿＿＿＿] made payable to Travel Publishing Ltd

Or:

Card No: [＿＿＿＿＿＿＿＿＿＿＿＿]

Expiry Date: [＿＿＿＿]

Signature: [＿＿＿＿＿＿＿＿＿＿＿]

NAME: [＿＿＿＿＿＿＿＿＿＿＿]

ADDRESS: [＿＿＿＿＿＿＿＿＿＿＿]

POSTCODE: [＿＿＿＿＿＿＿＿＿]

TEL NO· [＿＿＿＿＿＿＿＿＿]

Please either send or telephone your order to:

Travel Publishing Ltd
7a Apollo House
Calleva Park
Aldermaston
Berks, RG7 8TN

Tel : 0118 981 7777
Fax: 0118 982 0077

	PRICE	QUANTITY	VALUE

Hidden Places Regional Titles

Cambs & Lincolnshire	£7.99	....	....
Chilterns	£8.99	....	....
Cornwall	£8.99	....	....
Derbyshire	£7.99	....	....
Devon	£8.99	....	....
Dorset, Hants & Isle of Wight	£8.99	....	....
East Anglia	£8.99	....	....
Gloucestershire & Wiltshire	£7.99	....	....
Heart of England	£7.99	....	....
Hereford, Worcs & Shropshire	£7.99	....	....
Highlands & Islands	£7.99	....	....
Kent	£8.99	....	....
Lake District & Cumbria	£7.99	....	....
Lancashire & Cheshire	£8.99	....	....
Lincolnshire	£8.99	....	....
Northumberland & Durham	£8.99	....	....
Somerset	£7.99	....	....
Sussex	£7.99	....	....
Thames Valley	£7.99	....	....
Yorkshire	£7.99	....	....

Hidden Places National Titles

England	£9.99	....	....
Ireland	£9.99	....	....
Scotland	£9.99	....	....
Wales	£9.99	....	....

Hidden Inns Titles

West Country	£5.99	....	....
South East	£5.99	....	....
South	£5.99	....	....
South and Central Scotland	£5.99	....	....
Wales	£5.99	....	....

For orders of less than 4 copies please add £1 per book for postage & packing. Orders over 4 copies P & P free.

Hidden Places Order Form

To order any of our publications just fill in the payment details below and complete the order form *overleaf*. For orders of less than 4 copies please add £1 per book for postage and packing. Orders over 4 copies are P & P free.

Please Complete Either:

I enclose a cheque for £ [_____] made payable to Travel Publishing Ltd

Or:

Card No: [_____]

Expiry Date: [_____]

Signature: [_____]

NAME: [_____]

ADDRESS: [_____]

POSTCODE: [_____]

TEL NO: [_____]

Please either send or telephone your order to:

Travel Publishing Ltd
7a Apollo House
Calleva Park
Aldermaston
Berks, RG7 8TN

Tel : 0118 981 7777
Fax: 0118 982 0077

	PRICE	QUANTITY	VALUE

Hidden Places Regional Titles

	PRICE	QUANTITY	VALUE
Cambs & Lincolnshire	£7.99	....	....
Chilterns	£8.99	....	....
Cornwall	£8.99	....	....
Derbyshire	£7.99	....	....
Devon	£8.99	....	....
Dorset, Hants & Isle of Wight	£8.99	....	....
East Anglia	£8.99	....	....
Gloucestershire & Wiltshire	£7.99	....	....
Heart of England	£7.99	....	....
Hereford, Worcs & Shropshire	£7.99	....	....
Highlands & Islands	£7.99	....	....
Kent	£8.99	....	....
Lake District & Cumbria	£7.99	....	....
Lancashire & Cheshire	£8.99	....	....
Lincolnshire	£8.99	....	....
Northumberland & Durham	£8.99	....	....
Somerset	£7.99	....	....
Sussex	£7.99	....	....
Thames Valley	£7.99	....	....
Yorkshire	£7.99	....	....

Hidden Places National Titles

	PRICE	QUANTITY	VALUE
England	£9.99	....	....
Ireland	£9.99	....	....
Scotland	£9.99	....	....
Wales	£9.99	....	....

Hidden Inns Titles

	PRICE	QUANTITY	VALUE
West Country	£5.99	....	....
South East	£5.99	....	....
South	£5.99	....	....
South and Central Scotland	£5.99	....	....
Wales	£5.99	....	....

For orders of less than 4 copies please add £1 per book for
postage & packing. Orders over 4 copies P & P free.

Hidden Places Reader Reaction

The *Hidden Places* research team would like to receive reader's comments on any visitor attractions or places reviewed in the book and also recommendations for suitable entries to be included in the next edition. This will help ensure that the *Hidden Places* series continues to provide its readers with useful information on the more interesting, unusual or unique features of each attraction or place ensuring that their stay in the local area is an enjoyable and stimulating experience. To provide your comments or recommendations would you please complete the forms below and overleaf as indicated and send to:

The Research Department, Travel Publishing Ltd,
7a Apollo House, Calleva Park, Aldermaston, Reading, RG7 8TN.

Your Name:

Your Address:

Your Telephone Number:

Please tick as appropriate: Comments ☐ Recommendation ☐

Name of *"Hidden Place"*:

Address:

Telephone Number:

Name of Contact:

Hidden Places Reader Reaction

Comment or Reason for Recommendation:

....

....

....

....

....

....

....

....

....

....

....

Hidden Places Reader Reaction

The *Hidden Places* research team would like to receive reader's comments on any visitor attractions or places reviewed in the book and also recommendations for suitable entries to be included in the next edition. This will help ensure that the *Hidden Places* series continues to provide its readers with useful information on the more interesting, unusual or unique features of each attraction or place ensuring that their stay in the local area is an enjoyable and stimulating experience. To provide your comments or recommendations would you please complete the forms below and overleaf as indicated and send to:

The Research Department, Travel Publishing Ltd,
7a Apollo House, Calleva Park, Aldermaston, Reading, RG7 8TN.

Your Name:

Your Address:

Your Telephone Number:

Please tick as appropriate: Comments ☐   Recommendation ☐

Name of *"Hidden Place"*:

Address:

Telephone Number:

Name of Contact:

Hidden Places Reader Reaction

Comment or Reason for Recommendation:

....

....

....

....

....

....

....

....

....

....

....

Hidden Places Reader Reaction

The *Hidden Places* research team would like to receive reader's comments on any visitor attractions or places reviewed in the book and also recommendations for suitable entries to be included in the next edition. This will help ensure that the *Hidden Places* series continues to provide its readers with useful information on the more interesting, unusual or unique features of each attraction or place ensuring that their stay in the local area is an enjoyable and stimulating experience. To provide your comments or recommendations would you please complete the forms below and overleaf as indicated and send to:

The Research Department, Travel Publishing Ltd,

7a Apollo House, Calleva Park, Aldermaston, Reading, RG7 8TN.

Your Name:

Your Address:

Your Telephone Number:

Please tick as appropriate: Comments ☐ Recommendation ☐

Name of *"Hidden Place"*:

Address:

Telephone Number:

Name of Contact:

Hidden Places Reader Reaction

Comment or Reason for Recommendation:

....

....

....

....

....

....

....

....

....

....

....